The Rape of Nanking

The Nanjing Massacre That Occurred during the Second Sino-Japanese War

Free Bonus from Captivating History
(Available for a Limited time)

Hi History Lovers!

Now you have a chance to join our exclusive history list so you can get your first history ebook for free as well as discounts and a potential to get more history books for free! Simply visit the link below to join.

Captivatinghistory.com/ebook

Also, make sure to follow us on Facebook, Twitter and Youtube by searching for Captivating History.

Contents

Introduction

The Rape of Nanjing, also known as the Nanjing Massacre or the Nanking Massacre, was one of the most horrific atrocities of World War II, and it was perpetrated by the Japanese against the people of China who lived in the capital Nanjing. While most people have heard of the Holocaust, the history of the atrocities perpetrated in the East is far less known and is not often covered in schools. Similar to the Holocaust, the lives of citizens were completely disregarded as the invading Japanese military used them for a wide range of unethical actions. Reported activity includes experiments and competitions, with the competitions including members of the Japanese seeing who could kill the most people the fastest.

Unlike the Holocaust, the Nanjing Massacre only lasted six weeks, starting from the day the Japanese invaded the capital on December 13th, 1937. It is unknown exactly how many people were murdered during this time, but the estimates range from 40,000 unarmed combatants and civilians to more than 300,000. The invaders also sexually assaulted their victims. Like the Nazis, the Japanese stole from their victims as well, leaving the capital with valuables and priceless works of art.

It is difficult to know exactly what happened. Over the roughly six-week period, documents were kept by people who were in the city at the time, as well as by Japanese journalists. However, many of the documents were classified as secret by the Japanese government and stored so that the atrocities were not well known among the Japanese people. They were unable to keep other documents written by the Chinese and Westerners, though, so word spread throughout the rest of the world about what had happened. Before their final surrender, the Japanese military destroyed most of the documentation that they had kept on what happened, making it impossible to know exactly how many people were killed.

While it is easy to compare the Rape of Nanjing to the Holocaust, there are many notable differences as well, particularly in terms of how much is known. One of the reasons so much is known about the Holocaust is that the Allies actually walked into the concentration camps and saw the horrors that had been perpetrated against the people who were imprisoned within them. There were survivors who were able to tell the Allied liberators how they had been treated beyond the obvious starvation. People did survive the horrors of the Rape of Nanjing, but it had been more than seven years since the events of the atrocity, so most of the evidence of the horrors had already been destroyed. Many survivors were also not willing to relive the experience. In addition, those who were willing to talk about it did not have the kinds of details that people wanted to know, such as how many people were massacred.

Another reason why there isn't as much known about the six weeks of horror is due to the Cold War starting almost as soon as World War II ended. The US had largely been given control of helping to rebuild Japan, and they learned about some of the atrocities. However, they were more concerned with the potential threats posed by communist nations than in looking too far into the atrocity. The Chinese Civil War resumed once World War II ended, but regardless of which side won, the nation was going to be a communist one. Instead of seeking justice for the atrocities committed nearly a decade earlier, the US focused on building up Japan so that it would not fall to the potential threat of communism. That doesn't mean people were not held accountable, but justice was not sought on the same level against Japan as it was against Germany.

With so little attention being given to the Rape of Nanjing in the years following it, the horrors could have been completely forgotten. However, not everything was lost when the Japanese military destroyed much of their documentation. Many images of the military performing horrific acts and the carnage that they left on the beaches and in the city still remain.

War has always resulted in atrocities, but over the last one hundred years, record keeping and technology have made it easier to understand the extent of the horrors war can cause. The events of the Rape of Nanjing still remain a point of contention between Japan and China. The apologies issued by Japan are often seen by the Chinese as being either inadequate or insincere. The fact that some even dispute that it happened, despite the admission by some of the Japanese who were there and the images showing what happened, has further kept the nations from healing or establishing better relationships.

Chapter 1 – A Quick History of Sino-Japanese Relations

The relationship between China and Japan is called Sino-Japanese relations in English-speaking nations. Japan is an island nation located to the east of the main Asian continent, and it has had a unique relationship with the other continental nations. China is a large nation that makes up the majority of the eastern part of the continent. There are several small nations along the eastern border of the continent, including North Korea, South Korea, and Vietnam. Russia also touches the Pacific Ocean, taking up the majority of the northern part of Asia. All of these nations have maintained changing relationships over the centuries, making for a rich and complex history.

The relationship between Japan and China has always been unique. While China has broken apart and merged together over the centuries, Japan is one of the nations that China has never conquered. The conflicts between the two nations have long been a factor in their relationships with other empires and states in the region. However, the First Sino-Japanese War (1894–1895) significantly changed the dynamic between the two nations. Because of the Silk Road, China had strong ties to Europe, including familiarity with their weaponry. Japan had gone through a long period of isolationism, so they were learning about totally new technology. The Japanese quickly adapted, though, and during the short First Sino-Japanese War, Japan established itself as being far more dominant compared to its much larger neighbor.

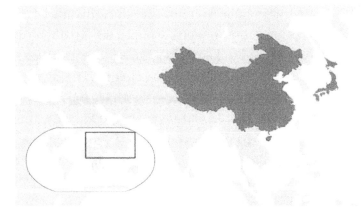

Map of China and Japan

https://commons.wikimedia.org/wiki/File:China_Japan_Locator.png

The First Sino-Japanese War

Both nations had placed claims on parts of what is now modern-day Korea. China had long controlled large portions of the area and relied on it as a client state, particularly because of all of its natural resources, like iron and coal. The land's natural resources were abundant enough to also attract Japan's attention. Japan, an island nation growing into the technology of the time, was seeking to trade with regions that could supply the resources it needed to modernize the country. With Korea being so close and rich in resources, the island nation began to consider ways that would allow it to make use of those resources. However, the territory was under China's control, making trade very limited. In an effort to improve trade, Japan started to encourage Korea to declare itself an independent nation, starting in 1875. The primary objective was to improve its own trade; Japan did not have any humanitarian interests when it helped to push the region to become self-sufficient and independent from Chinese rule. By working directly with a new nation instead of having to work with China, Japan would have been able to establish agreements that were more beneficial to their own self-interests.

Both nations favored different portions of the Korean government, with Japan backing the more radical and forward-looking officials who wanted to make the region more modern. China supported the more traditional officials who wanted to keep things largely the way they had always been. The tension these two nations created within the Korean government began to adversely affect it, and in 1884, the group that wanted to reform the region, the side aligned with the Japanese, made its move to overthrow the Korean government. China had military officials in the region, and they swiftly sent their military in to save the king and support the administration. During the ensuing battle, some Japanese legation members were killed. The only reason that war did not begin between China and Japan at this point was due to a mutual agreement to remove all of their troops, an agreement they reached and signed at the Li-Ito Convention.

Over the next five years, Japan was able to make significant strides in its efforts to modernize the nation. In 1894, the Japanese were feeling considerable national pride at how rapidly they had managed to achieve their goals. This pride seemed to have spread to the younger Korean people, who saw the changes and were inspired. China reacted with apparent apprehension, and they invited the Korean leader of the coup of 1884, Kim Ok-gyun, to Shanghai. Once there, Kim Ok-gyun was assassinated. His body was returned and displayed, likely as a reminder to the Koreans that they were still a part of China.

Japan did not take this obvious affront well, and even its citizens were angered at how China had found a way to go back on the agreement. China had not sent its military into Korea, opting instead to lure a high-profile pro-Japanese figure and assassinate him. That same year, the Tonghak rebellion began, resulting in the Korean king requesting assistance from China to put it down. When China complied, Japan saw this as a violation of the Li-Ito Convention. They sent eight thousand of their own troops. China then responded by sending more troops on the British steamer *Kowshing*, which the Japanese sank. War was inevitable, and it was officially declared on August 1ˢᵗ, 1894. Most of the world expected China to easily defeat Japan. They had been modernizing their nation for much longer, and they were a much larger nation. However, everyone underestimated just how much work Japan had done. Though it was a much smaller and less populous country, it was better prepared for the war. Japan had largely won the war by the beginning of March 1895, as the Japanese quickly executed several overwhelming victories against China, both in the water and on land. They had invaded both Manchuria and the Shandong province, giving them posts that helped them to control the waters. This meant that, for the Chinese, reaching Beijing by sea was much harder, and it was a blow that China could not accept. China sought peace soon after, and the Treaty of Shimonoseki was soon initiated. As a result, Korea was given its independence, although it had to cede the Liaodong Peninsula, the Pescadores, and Taiwan. Japan established itself as a much larger player on the world's stage, having accomplished what most considered to be impossible—easily executing a decisive defeat against the much larger, more historically open China.

Relations Following the War

Having seen that China could be defeated, and by a small nation at that, European nations were inspired to push China for more change. Internally, China began to look to do more to become more modern. Changes were made to the Treaty of Shimonoseki when European nations began to worry about Japan expanding, with Russia (a nation that was just across a small body of water from Japan) playing a large role in pressing for these changes. Russia had long wanted the peninsula that China had been required to give to Japan, and both France and Germany felt that Japan was enough of a threat to warrant relinquishing the lands. Japan ended up selling the region to Russia, but this intervention by the European powers caused some resentment in Japan, especially among the people in the military. Eventually, that resentment caused the Russo-Japanese War (1904–1905) to break out, which ended with another Japanese victory.

By the early part of the 20th century, Japan had established itself as a much more important nation on the global stage. The First Sino-Japanese War resulted in the island nation starting to form its own empire, and the Russo-Japanese War helped to further expand that empire. This inspired the Japanese to attempt to take more lands and take a much more aggressive approach in increasing its influence.

With these two major successes within a decade, a sense of nationalism and superiority began to grow in Japan, particularly within the military. Intellectuals and members of the military began to believe that such quick, decisive victories against two much larger, more powerful nations were a sign that they were destined to control a much larger chunk of the world. The historian Kurakichi Shiratori best explained this sentiment as "Nothing in the world compares to the divine nature of the imperial house and likewise the majesty of our national polity. Here is one great reason for Japan's superiority."

This sentiment is incredibly familiar to anyone who has studied the first half of the 20th century (or any other period in history that deals with empires). Nationalism was spreading across Europe as well, in an equally detrimental way, resulting in the start of World War I. A series of tragedies resulted in nations being dragged one by one into the war until it engulfed all of the European continent. However, because of the empire-building that the European nations had been enacting over the years, nations from around the world were pulled into the fight. France and Great Britain were the primary nations on the one side, while Germany was the primary nation on the opposite side. Russia was not a part of the war for long because the nation fell into a civil war, called the Bolshevik Revolution, which resulted in the assassination of the entire Russian royal family.

When the war first erupted in Europe, both China and Japan saw it as an opportunity to remove European influence from Asia. As a result, both nations declared war on Germany. China had continued to lose lands after the First Sino-Japanese War, but the losses were to European nations (France had a settlement in Shanghai, and England took over Hong Kong). It is likely that they hoped to negotiate with these nations after helping them to beat Germany. However, China had other reasons to declare war on Germany, for the nation had attacked the city of Qingdao in 1897 under the guise of seeking justice for two German missionaries killed in the city.

China offered to help Great Britain, but the offer was declined. It wouldn't be accepted until 1916 that the British prime minister tried to persuade the nation that they needed the help. Japan quickly spoke up, saying that it did not agree with China being so actively involved in the war. If China was to participate successfully, it would threaten Japan's status in Asia. In an effort to avoid an all-out war with Japan, China decided to send non-military personnel to help with the fight in Britain, France, and Russia (they remained a part of the war in a minor capacity after the Bolsheviks took over the nation). The support staff helped in manufacturing, repairs, and transport.

Japan ended up successfully taking Qingdao in 1915, then issued the Twenty-One Demands to China. This set of demands required that China give up even more land. It is likely that China hoped that its efforts to help Europe would result in reclaiming some of the lost lands.

Toward the end of World War I, the United States finally joined the conflict, and it had a goal of finally resolving the question of which nation would control the disputed areas. China finally made its declaration of war against Germany in 1917 in the hopes of garnering more support from the US once the war ended. By the war's end, China had both the longest-serving and largest contingent of non-European workers in Europe. The Chinese had been planning for the end of the war since 1915, so they were eager to have their representatives push for the restoration of the mainland under their control. Those hopes were quickly dashed, though, as the Paris Peace Conference saw only two seats at the conference given to China, while five were given to Japan. The justification for this was that Japan had actually supplied troops. European nations considered the Twenty-One Demands as something that should be honored in order to resolve the claim to the lands. Of all the nations to attend the Paris Peace Conference, China was the only one that refused to sign the Treaty of Versailles.

As a result of the slight and the perceived rejection of their sovereignty by the most powerful European and North American nations, China began to reevaluate its position. In 1921, this led to the formation of the Chinese Communist Party and a long civil war. While China entered a long period of turmoil as it tried to find its place in the world, Japan continued to look for ways to take over larger portions of continental Asia.

Chapter 2 – A Brief History of Nanjing

Nanjing (once better known as Nanking) has an extensive history, making it difficult to know how many of the stories that have survived are true and how many are myths. There are two primary stories told about the city. The first indicates that Nanjing is over 2,600 years. The small settlement, which was founded around 571 BCE, developed into a much larger city over the millennia. When people first began settling in the area, they coalesced around Tangyi, a tiny village. Today, this is located on the western side of the city.

The second story of the city's founding places the date around 472 BCE. According to this version, the head of state, Goujian, had the city built near the southwestern area of the modern-day Zhonghua Gate. At that time, the city was known as Yue City. The construction of the city included walls to protect the residents, making it one of the oldest fortified locations in China. It is also the oldest place in modern-day Nanjing (though it took up a much smaller part of the city since it was considerably smaller over two thousand years ago).

It is possible that both of these stories are true, with the main distinction being that it was only a village and that it didn't officially become a city until 472 BCE when the walls were constructed around it.

In 229 CE, King Sun Quan made it the capital of the Kingdom of Wu, though, at the time, the city was named Jianye. Before this time, the capital of the kingdom had been in the Yellow River region. As a result of the shift, the southern part of the kingdom began to thrive and change, attracting a lot more people. It remained the capital of the Kingdom of Wu through five Chinese dynasties. Between 229 and 589 CE, the name was changed from Jianye to Jiankang, though it is unknown when the change became official. During the time when it was called Jiankang, it became the world's largest city, and it was likely the first city to have over one million people. During this time, it would have been comparable to Rome at its height, and it was considered by many to be the cultural center of the world. It was a hub for many industries and trade, including architecture and marine trade. It also saw the development and growth of a number of Asian religions, including Buddhism, Confucianism, and Taoism.

After having prospered over three hundred years, the capital began an inevitable decline; all cities go through decline, but it was rebuilt again later. The primary reason for the city's descent was the presence of separatists, particularly the ones near the capital. The capital was moved, and Jinling (yet another name given to the city) was converted to a prefecture (equivalent to a county). While the city was no longer as prominent, it remained a hub for culture and scholars who wanted to study the empire's history.

After China divided under the period called the Five Dynasties and Ten Kingdoms, Jinling once again became the capital, though only of the region. This time, the focus was on building the three primary pillars of culture: agriculture, art, and commerce.

By the time the Ming dynasty was established in 1368 CE, the city had been renamed Nanjing. Under the first member of the Ming dynasty, Zhu Yuanzhang, the city was made the capital of the dynasty. Though Nanjing was not as populous as it had been a few hundred years earlier, it did become the largest city in the country, with an estimated 700,000 people residing in and around it. This time, though, the city began attracting attention from outside of the country. Students came to Nanjing to study, particularly from Korea, Japan, and Vietnam. Even after the capital was shifted to the port city of Beijing in 1421, Nanjing continued to function as the auxiliary capital. The population once again boomed, and as a result, Nanjing became the world's most populous capital city. It was even compared to the most extravagant European nations by those who traveled between the two continents.

The city continued to experience a boom for several hundred years, becoming a culturally significant place for art and commerce. It became an important part of the silk trade, and it was also the setting for one of the most popular classic Chinese novels, *Hong Lou Meng* (*Dream of the Red Mansions*).

One of the most disgraceful periods for the city occurred as a result of the Opium Wars during the Qing dynasty. The dynasty reached an agreement with Great Britain called the Treaty of Nanjing. This appeared to be a significant loss for the city and China, as the terms set forth in the treaty made China more like a semi-colony of the European nation. It gave Great Britain a much greater say in tariffs, commercial preference, and consular jurisdiction. This is considered to be the beginning of modern China, for it was around this time that the nation began to modernize.

In an effort to make up for the large sums of money that the nation had spent during the Opium Wars, the Chinese government heavily taxed the citizens (or perhaps more accurately to erase the savings, as the nation became more feudalistic following the signing of the treaty). This resulted in peasant wars, as the people felt wronged by the government. During this unrest, the Taiping army saw an opportunity to take control of Nanjing. The army was created by Hong Xiuquan in

1837. He was the son of a peasant family but had received a classical education that taught him about beliefs from around the world. After failing to gain work in the imperial court, Hong became ill, then fell into a coma. Upon waking, he claimed to have had a vision that he was Jesus's younger brother and that he needed to lead people to establish a "Heavenly Kingdom of Great Peace." This was to be done through war with the emperor and those who supported the emperor, especially the military. By 1853, his army was much larger than the emperor's. Hong Xiuquan's men took control of Nanjing, but they were not able to control it for long. The Taiping Rebellion lasted for thirteen years, and when it ended, the Taiping army was finally put down. However, it also proved to be the end of the Qing dynasty.

By 1912, China was reasserting itself on the world stage, having modernized more than most of the other Eastern nations (except for Japan). On the first day of 1912, the Provisional Government of the Republic of China was formed in Nanjing.

The years between 1927 and 1937 are considered to be a golden period for the city because it was when the nation established its major infrastructure, on which most of the city still currently runs. However, it was this prominence, wealth of resources, and cultural importance that made the city a desirable target to the Japanese. With Europe already embroiled in war and Japan having made advances in continental Asia, the Japanese were looking for a place that would give them greater dominance farther inland while also helping to increase their resources. The Japanese thought that if they were able to successfully take Nanjing with its impressive municipal infrastructure, they would establish better footing within China. It would also be a significant blow to the divided Chinese government, as the civil war would have made the large nation too weak to face invasions. The loss of Nanjing would significantly reduce Chinese morale.

Even today, the city plays an important role in China. The name Nanjing has become more popular over the last few decades, but Nanjing and Nanking are used interchangeably. The difference is mostly based on how the Chinese characters translate into Western letters. For the sake of consistency, this book will use Nanjing; however, if you are interested in learning more, Nanking tends to be used more often in historical context based on Western interpretation. Nanjing is the standardized version adapted during the 1950s as the preferred Eastern spelling.

Chapter 3 – Japan's Invasion of China

The start of the Second Sino-Japanese War was very similar to how tensions across Europe were built. Germany was able to acquire control over other nations through increasingly hostile tactics. The way Japan began to take over portions of Asia was similar because it initially started by stating claims over regions with largely questionable rights. By 1937, all pretense of a civil acquisition was gone, as Japan had become openly hostile, invading nations without any rights to their land.

Japanese Control of Manchuria

Japan had been exercising control over Manchuria due to its dubious claim over the region from the Twenty-One Demands. When Europe failed to restore the region to China, the country found itself in a poor position to try to reclaim Manchuria. With the Republic of China still working to form a government and with different divisions fighting for power, Japan was able to gain a much better foothold on the continent.

In 1931, Japan began to move farther into the region. On September 18th, they created an incident at the South Manchurian Railway to justify moving into Manchuria and occupying it, a move that was against the treaty they had signed with China. When part of the railroad was destroyed in an explosion, the Japanese declared it was an attack by the Chinese, pointing to the local garrison as the perpetrators of the explosion. Japan quickly moved into the area. The local government refused to fight, essentially letting the Japanese take control over a large portion of the province.

The leaders of China were unable to send anyone to fight the Japanese, so they turned to the League of Nations in the hopes that it would help. The harshest thing that the League of Nations did was to demand that the Japanese withdraw from the area by November 16th, 1931. Japan, particularly its military, dismissed this resolution. The League of Nations had no follow-up measures against the Japanese when they refused to leave. The US did pass the Stimson Doctrine, which said that the country would not recognize Japan's claim since it ignored China's sovereignty in the region.

With little action to actually dissuade them, the Japanese established their own puppet government over the region, which they renamed Manchukuo. At the head of the government was Puyi, the last emperor of China. Though this gave the appearance of legitimacy, the League of Nations quickly took the same stance as the US and refused to acknowledge the puppet government. With so many seeming to turn on them, Japan left the League of Nations in March 1933, a move that Germany would mirror that October. With the failure of the League to act to save members of its own organization from others within it, this was the beginning of the end for the organization. As remaining members lost faith in its ability, the League of Nations stopped playing any role in securing its member nations, and it finally dissolved in 1946.

Though Hitler was rising to power in Germany and the European nations were becoming increasingly aggressive, it was Japan's actions in Manchuria that would start the chain of events that would ultimately lead to the dissolution of many of the measures put in place after World War I. Before the next major movements in China took place, Japan, Italy, Spain, and Germany formed their own pact since they no longer belonged to the League of Nations.

During the Japanese occupation of Nanjing, many of the atrocities were committed on the Chinese people. However, with Japan controlling the narrative and the region and with no one to talk about the horrors, there is less documentation and stories about how the Manchurians were treated.

Start of the Second Sino-Japanese War: The Marco Polo Bridge Incident

It took a few years before Japan would act again. Their move to take over Manchuria had not resulted in any real action against them, but other nations were displeased. By biding their time, the Japanese were able to build up more forces on the continent. By 1937, the military had finished their preparations, so Japan began to move on to other regions, including Beijing, Shanghai, and eventually Nanjing.

Following so much unrest and this thinly veiled power grab in the name of expanding their empire, the Japanese ceased hiding their intent in 1937. Japanese soldiers were conducting exercises about thirty miles from Beijing, but they had not notified the Chinese, something that had traditionally been done to establish intent and prevent war. The exercises were taking place near the Marco Polo Bridge. When it was over, the Japanese claimed that they had lost a soldier, and in return, they demanded that the Chinese soldiers allow them to enter Wanping, a nearby town, to look for him. When the Chinese refused to let them into their territory, the Japanese began to force their way to the town. Both nations reacted by sending troops to bolster their numbers.

The exercise startled the Chinese troopers who were stationed close to the training exercises, which resulted in a brief skirmish. Initially, Japan was able to take control of the bridge, but that was short-lived. At the end of the day on July 8th, only four of the one hundred estimated Chinese defenders survived the attacks of the Imperial Army. Japan controlled the bridge until the next morning when Chinese reinforcements arrived and reclaimed it.

The next morning, the tension built until the two sides began fighting at the bridge. The Chinese quickly took control, forcing the Japanese to pull back, and they established a short-lived verbal agreement. According to that agreement, China would issue an apology for what had happened, but military leaders on both sides would be punished for the incident. China would also replace the military troops with civilians who belonged to the Peace Preservation Corps. Japan was to pull back from the area. The agreement was signed on July 11th.

This minor incident seemed to have been easily resolved, but the way it was portrayed back in Japan would cause tensions to escalate. The Japanese Cabinet held a press conference and appeared to reassure the people that things were fine by announcing that both sides had reached an agreement. However, they also announced that they were mobilizing three new divisions in their army and issued a warning to the governing body in Nanjing that it should refrain from interfering with the solution that both sides had reached. Given that Japan was mobilizing to the region, Nanjing responded by sending out four divisions. With both sides clearly breaking the agreement, hostilities quickly began. On July 20th, Japan attacked Wanping, shelling the city, and by the end of the month, the Imperial Army had surrounded both Beijing and Tianjin. With two important cities under their control, Japan turned its eyes to the historically significant capital city of Nanjing. However, it was the assassination of one of Japan's naval officers at the beginning of August 1937 that would finally lead to the declaration of war. At the time, it was called the Second Sino-Japanese War, as Europe was still maintaining a delicate peace. However, it wouldn't be long before Japan and Germany would make their interests very clear as they took over nations around them.

Sanko-Sakusen: Planning to Invade Nanjing and the Three Alls Policy

Like the Nazis, the Japanese had a slogan that helped to dictate their actions during the war: Sanko-Sakusen. However, the Japanese did not create concentration camps and then put the motto over the camps' gates (most German concentration camps "welcomed" the prisoners with the slogan *Arbeit Macht Frei*, which translates to "Work Sets You Free."). Instead, the Japanese military followed a policy described as the "Three Alls": "Kill all. Burn all. Loot all." In the West, this is comparable to scorched earth tactics, which would be executed by the Soviets later in World War II as they retreated from the Germans. However, the Soviets were not trying to take over lands but rather destroy all potential resources, leaving the Germans with nothing to take but scorched earth. It was incredibly effective against the Germans, as it eventually meant they had to stretch their supply lines too long and too thin. Unfortunately, it was equally effective when used by the Japanese, but it also meant the slaughter of hundreds of thousands to millions of civilians wherever the Imperial Army went.

Japan would establish concentration camps, even creating a place that has come to be known as China's Auschwitz. However, the Japanese government didn't send people to a single location the way the Nazis did. More often, they would simply slaughter people where they lived. Ironically, when Japan took control of Manchuria, the Japanese wanted to populate the region with Jewish people fleeing from Europe, giving refuge to the people that Japan's allies were trying to exterminate. The area already had a large European Jewish population because many Hebrews had fled from Russia in the middle of the previous century. Japan helped Jewish people flee across Russia to settle in Japanese-controlled lands, and many saw this as a humanitarian project. Japan did stand to benefit, especially as there were many engineers, bankers, and other well-educated people looking for sanctuary. Still, it was clearly an affront to one of Japan's few political allies. The Japanese also did not seem to think of the Jewish refugees as equals. The plan to settle them was known as the Fugu Plan because they saw the Jewish refugees as being similar to pufferfish (known as fugu in Japanese): they are delightful when handled right but toxic if handled wrong.

The term Sanko-Sakusen was used by Japanese soldiers who discussed their actions nearly two decades later in 1957. They admitted to committing atrocities and acknowledged the ideologies behind their own horrific actions. Many of them pointed to indoctrination, which had children learning to idolize the emperor and military, resulting in obedience in doing what they were told. The idea that people of other nations were lesser made many Japanese soldiers look at the civilians more as objects than people, which allowed them to commit horrific acts without feeling regret. It would be a similar sentiment expressed by the Germans, although they primarily said that they simply didn't question orders because most of Europe no longer had the same sense of a beloved monarch or emperor by the 1930s and 1940s.

Over the first six months of the Second Sino-Japanese War, Japan had taken control of Tianjin, Beijing, and Shanghai. The Chinese people who survived told of the atrocities that had been committed up to the Imperial Army's arrival, though most of the atrocities were focused on quashing the Chinese as quickly as possible. Since these areas had a larger Western population (cities in port areas often had larger populations of Western citizens for business reasons, as well as members of the military to protect areas under the control of Western nations), the Japanese seemed to be more measured in their approach to dealing with citizens and prisoners of war. As Chinese leaders saw their land and port cities begin to be taken by the invaders, they did not ignore the warning signs. Knowing that Japan would move on Nanjing, China was faced with making a decision about how to react. With little time to make their move, the Chinese would make the only move they felt they could.

Chapter 4 – The Second Battle of Shanghai and Building Frustration and Resentment toward the Chinese

Between 1931 and 1937, China remained divided as the Nationalist Party and the Chinese Communist Party fought for control over the country. Even as anti-Japanese sentiment grew in the country, neither side was willing to stop their internal struggle until the Japanese began to take control of some of their most important cities in 1937. Following the slaughter at Shanghai, the Chinese would look for ways to save the people in their capital city as the Japanese turned their attention south.

No Good Options

Though China had been able to modernize, in large part because of the help it had received from Germany over the years since the end of World War I, the nation had been fighting a civil war for years by 1937. They knew that they could not beat the Japanese as they began to march farther into China. The two sides trying to run the government began to consider what they could do, knowing that they didn't have many good options available.

With the Japanese pouring in from their island and the other lands they controlled, particularly Manchuria, China decided its best option was to pull its resources and as many people as possible from the coastal area and move them away from the cities in the eastern part of the country. Just like Russia would do several years later, China would eventually adopt a scorched earth policy, destroying any potential resources that the Japanese might be able to use. This would be just as effective a method against the Japanese, who lived on an island that lacked those resources, as it would be against the Germans, who didn't have the proper resources and supplies for the harsh Russian winters.

In 1937, the Chinese began to move whatever they could from the cities, but the speed with which the Japanese attacked would make it difficult to make any substantial progress. At this time, the Chinese did not know the kinds of horrors that the Japanese would enact, nor would they adapt the scorched earth policy until they lost their important eastern cities.

Attack on Shanghai

After their success in taking over Manchuria in 1932, the Japanese attacked Shanghai. The Chinese had fought hard, losing many soldiers to the attack, but they had the verbal support of most of Europe (including Great Britain, which still kept troops in the area) and the US. Japan continued to send troops to the region, finally building a force of more than 100,000 men by the end of February 1932. They were about to defeat the Chinese forces in the areas around the city, but their victory was short-lived, as the Chinese forces in the city pushed back the invaders. The Imperial forces continued to attack at the beginning of March, and even though the Chinese forces that remained in the area were considered elite (the 87th and 88th Divisions had been trained by the Germans), they could not withstand the continued attacks by Japan. Europe and the US played small roles, but they helped to work out a ceasefire, giving Japan control over much of the area. This further angered the Chinese, but there was little they could do. This came to be known as the First Battle of Shanghai, and it set the stage for a much larger war just a few years later.

In 1937, the Japanese had established a much better foothold in the region, and they would soon begin the major initiative of the Second Sino-Japanese War. Up to this point, the fights had been on a much smaller scale. However, the Second Battle of Shanghai, also known as the Battle of Songhu, would make it impossible to restore peace.

The tension that had been building since 1932 reached a peak on August 9th, 1937, when First Lieutenant Isao Oyama tried to enter Shanghai's Hungchiao Airport, which was a breach of the signed agreement. The Chinese opened fire on him, killing the Japanese soldier. While apologizing for their officer's actions, the Japanese demanded the disarmament of the Chinese Peace Preservation Corps. When Japanese soldiers arrived in Shanghai to see to this disarmament, the Chinese refused. Based on the previous actions of the Japanese, the Chinese likely suspected that the disarmament was a precursor to war. If the Chinese soldiers were disarmed, they would then be much easier for the Japanese soldiers to defeat. Since it was their soldier who had been in the wrong, as he had broken the agreement, it made no sense for the Chinese to be the ones to disarm. Small clashes occurred in the city, and the Japanese troops requested reinforcements. When the Chinese military leader in Shanghai, General Zhang Zhizhong, learned of the Japanese request, he also asked that reinforcements be sent to support his troops.

Western leaders attempted to cool these tensions because open war would harm their interests in the area. Some nations had control over small areas in the region, while others had significant commercial and industrial interests that would be disrupted if the two strongest Asian powers were unable to come to peaceful terms.

The Japanese soldiers made their move on August 13th at nine in the morning by marching ten thousand troops into the Shanghai suburbs. The Chinese troops began attacking the invaders by the afternoon. The invaders, who launched airstrikes and sent in additional troops against the Chinese fighters, hoped to be able to finish the fight in about three days. General Zhang Zhizhong was able to drag the fight out to about three months. Unfortunately, the Chinese forces were simply unable to repel the Japanese. What Zhang had done was to allow time for some of the Chinese citizens to escape and to remove as many resources from the city as possible. Since the fighting occurred around three strategic areas (within the downtown area, in the towns around the city, and along the Jiangsu coast), the Japanese were unable to focus their attacks on one area, making it so the Japanese could not prevent the flow of people and industries from the city. With the fight going on longer than they had expected and with Japanese troops executing actions that their officers considered dishonorable (including many of the actions that the soldiers would take in Nanjing after it had fallen, just on a much smaller scale) to finish the fight as fast as possible, the Japanese felt a significant blow to their morale. The heavy loss of troops further demoralized the Japanese, but they ultimately won. After fighting in and around Shanghai for seventy-five days, the Chinese began to withdraw from the downtown area. The best fighters remained behind to hold off the Japanese, and the Chinese lost roughly 60 percent of those men. Initially, they had hoped for reinforcements, but they never arrived. However, the elite forces did help to ensure that the Chinese were able to prevent the Japanese from making use of their resources from the city. They also slowed down the timeline for Japan to begin their push farther south to Nanjing.

It is estimated that roughly 300,000 Chinese lost their lives during the battle, compared to the roughly 40,000 Japanese soldiers who died. It is likely that this serious loss of life significantly affected how the two sides viewed each other. Some think this could have contributed to the animosity and cruelty that followed the battle. However, given the medical facilities that were created to experiment on the Chinese soldiers (facilities that rival the human experiments of the Nazis) and the Three Alls Policy, the Japanese would have enacted atrocities even if they had managed to take the city in the planned timeframe.

The Western Witnesses of the Battle

Shanghai had been difficult to take in part because Western nations had created their own little havens within the city. There was a region in the city called the International Settlement. Shanghai was the second-largest Asian city (Tokyo was the largest), and it was a port for nations that had territories in Asia. When the Japanese attacked, Western citizens and military personnel witnessed the fight. They largely remained neutral as the two Asian nations fought for control of the city and surrounding areas. Ironically, the Japanese were one of the largest populations of civilians in the International Settlement. This could have helped contribute to the reluctance by Western nations to react, as they had largely seen the Japanese in a very different light outside of their military aspirations.

However, when the Japanese attacked civilians, some of the Western soldiers intervened, most notably working to help Chinese civilians who were trapped to get away from the invaders. However, they never directly fought the Japanese and largely left the Chinese to their fate. Considering how much difficulty they were having back on the continent, it is likely that the Westerners were attempting to avoid dividing their forces across two continents. They did see firsthand just how brutal the Japanese soldiers could be, but their presence likely kept the Japanese from committing the same kinds of atrocities they would in Nanjing.

A Hint of the Horrors to Come

When it was clear that the Chinese were either retreating or surrendering, the Japanese were merciless toward the soldiers they captured. Many of the Chinese soldiers who were still in the city went into the International Settlement to surrender instead of giving themselves up to the Japanese. Outside of the city, the invaders began to show how they were going to operate for the next few months. Even those who remained in the city weren't safe.

To help boost the soldiers' spirits, the Japanese troops forced many of the women who were still in the city to become "comfort women," essentially forcing them into sexual slavery. This was not the first time they had done that either; Chinese women in Manchuria had been forced to provide whatever the Japanese soldiers had wanted after the takeover roughly five years earlier. The practice was established after the Manchurian Incident at the request of military authorities, and as a result, brothels were opened to entertain men stationed in the region. The establishment of these brothels was documented, giving historians a better look at how the practice of comfort women began. The practice had been introduced in Shanghai after the first battle, with the first official station being made at the naval brigade near the city. At the time, it was thought that the establishment of these kinds of facilities would keep the soldiers from raping Chinese women in the area, which would build resentment of the Japanese. It was also meant to help reduce the spread of sexually transmitted diseases, as there was control over the women who were "comforting" the soldiers. This means that by the Second Battle of Shanghai, there were already brothels for the soldiers. However, at the beginning of 1938, when the leaders in Shanghai requested three thousand Japanese women to come "serve" the Imperial Army, perception in Japan shifted. The people accused the military of abducting women and tarnishing the public image and honor of the soldiers, so the use of Japanese women in the brothels dwindled. As there were regulations on which women could be brought from Japan in the early part of 1938, the military forced women from other nations into the brothels, including from Korea and Taiwan. While the war began before these regulations were established, opinion back in Japan had already turned, so the military had likely found other ways to ensure that their men were "comforted" with a lot less scrutiny from the citizens back home.

The Second Battle of Shanghai finally ended in the middle of November. By November 19th, the Japanese were pushing to keep the Chinese on the run, and they planned to force their adversaries toward Nanjing. Lieutenant General Yanagawa Heisuke had been the one to send word back to the Imperial Headquarters to begin the move south, but the military leaders appointed General Matsui Iwane to be the commander-in-chief. When Matsui fell ill, the emperor's uncle, Lieutenant General Prince Asaka Yasuhiko, became the commander of the force.

The events at Shanghai were actually similar to what was to come, both in Asia and in Europe. Historians often correlate the battles in Asia with the battles in Europe. For instance, the Second Battle of Shanghai has been called the Asian Stalingrad. One of the main differences was that most of the primary players in the war were present in Asia for the first major battle of what would become World War II.

Chapter 5 – War Crimes Committed on the Way to Nanjing

The Nanjing Massacre is often discussed, and it covered a period of about six weeks, but the atrocities that were committed by the Imperial Army began before they even left Shanghai. As the soldiers moved between the port city to the capital, they released their anger, aggression, and feeling of superiority on the people they encountered. Japanese journalists were often embedded within the military to relay information about how impressive the military was and how easily they crushed their enemies. One of these reporters recorded his impressions at the time, saying that the reason they were able to move so quickly was that they were able to do whatever they wanted along the way. They raped women they encountered and looted settlements. This was condoned, and some have reported it was even encouraged by many of those in charge.

Several books have been written about the period between the attack on Shanghai and the events of Nanjing because it is often overlooked. While the death toll was not as high during this time, the Japanese showed no mercy during the march.

Stories of a Callous Competition

One story that arose during this time revolved around a competition between two officers. According to the story, the two officers strove to see who could kill one hundred people the fastest using just a sword. Journalists sent stories back about the competition, likely as a way to help build support for the military. However, there is a question about how true this story actually was. The way that the alleged events were covered was more of a sporting event. Since the count was for one hundred men, it was not a competition that could be completed within a day. This meant that there was a daily account of these events as the men worked to get to the designated number of kills. Given what would happen in Nanjing, there are many people who believe that these accounts were true, that two men really did try to see who the most efficient killer was. However, there has been a lot of debate and doubt cast on the stories reported back to the Japanese citizens. Those who don't believe that the stories were real have argued that it was likely reporters were working to build pride in the military and heighten support. According to this theory, it was the soldiers who made up all of the stories. It would likely have helped to build their morale after the difficulties in Shanghai.

With many people having fled from Shanghai to Nanjing, many of the people who lived between the two cities likely fled as well. It would have been very obvious where the Imperial Army would go after their success in the major port city. Word of how the Japanese had treated the Chinese in and around Shanghai would likely have made it difficult to find many remaining Chinese people along the route, though not all of them would have the ability to flee. After all, the way many of the more rural Chinese were treated during the civil war was atrocious. There were reports of the Chinese leaders forcing their citizens into slave labor in some regions, particularly near the port cities. While many of the people between Shanghai and Nanjing weren't subjected to forced labor, they likely would not have had the money to leave. It is difficult to know how many people lived between the two cities because census information is not available.

The authenticity of the news reports about this particular competition is uncertain, but the details definitely originated within the military, even if it was just the soldiers coming up with tales to try to raise support back home. This showed a callousness toward the Chinese, especially if such tales would boost morale. It also helped to cement the frame of mind the soldiers were in when they headed toward Nanjing. The fact that they could so easily dispatch people and see it as a competition (whether or not it happened) indicates how the idea of the warrior was translated to then modern-day settings.

The Warrior Code and Indoctrination

For a long stretch of Japanese history, samurai were an honorable class and were considered among the elite, both in the military and in daily life. By the early part of the 20th century, the class of samurai had changed, and they largely helped to control the direction of the nation, particularly the growth and rapid expansion of the military. The idea of creating a Japanese empire appealed to the former samurai class. However, the change in weaponry made it easier to enlist a much wider group of soldiers. Lower social classes had always been a part of the military, but now, the leaders had much larger groups under their control. Though the samurai class was no longer a part of Japanese society, there was still a lot of respect for their actions, and soldiers bought swords that were either antique or similar to samurai swords. These swords were taken into battle so that soldiers would be able to commit suicide instead of being dishonored by defeat.

The need to fight for the emperor was impressed upon the citizens, and boys were able to enlist when they were just fourteen years old. While it was said that they fought for the emperor, it was largely the military that pulled the strings. By bringing such young boys into fighting, they were able to more completely indoctrinate them, something that many have compared to brainwashing. Death was considered to be the most honorable end, and this ideology was mixed with the older way of the warrior, a code for how samurai were to behave that was called Bushido. Some of the most extreme practices under this code included seppuku (committing suicide to atone for a failure or loss) and kamikaze (largely practiced by pilots who sacrificed themselves to kill as many of their enemies as possible). However, many other components of that code were ignored during the march between Shanghai and Nanjing. Bushido requires that a warrior be courageous, practice self-denial, and be loyal to their lord (during the 1930s, this had become the emperor).

Some have pointed to this code and how it was used during the 1930s and 1940s to indicate the soldiers' states of mind, but the comparison between the code and the actions of the soldiers at this time were significantly different. This is more obvious when going over the documentation of the events and how fervently some Japanese have denied that they even happened.

The mindset of the men by the time they reached the city was likely one of extreme patriotism and a desire to prove themselves. Due to ideas of being superior to the people around them, a negative view of women from other nations, and the idea that they were trying to prove themselves, the Japanese soldiers were in a mindset that likely contributed to the events that began once the soldiers entered the city as victors. It would not take them nearly as long to defeat the Chinese soldiers in Nanjing as it did in Shanghai, in large part because the Chinese had already evacuated all of their important figures. Citizens who could not afford to move and lower-level soldiers were left behind to face the invaders who had become agitated as they marched toward Nanjing.

Chapter 6 – The Order to Kill

The orders that were given are not entirely known because many of the accounts were given when the Japanese were put on trial for war crimes years after the war ended. The accounts given were varied, which could indicate the different experiences of the soldiers. Three men controlled large troops of men, and they each advanced on the city from different directions. General Matsui Iwane had been appointed the commander general, and he led an amphibious group. Nakajima Kesago was the leader of a large group of men who moved along the southern banks of the famous Yangtze River; this group came from the west. Lieutenant General Yanagawa Heisuke was responsible for the third group, which moved toward the city from the southeast.

Each of these leaders had a different approach to the war, and they likely inspired very different emotions from their soldiers.

- General Matsui Iwane was responsible for the attack on the city, and he was a well-respected leader within the military. He was a firm Buddhist and came from a family of scholars, and he seemed to try to live by these principles prior to the war. He had retired from the military but was called up to fight in August 1937.

- Nakajima Kesago has been described as cruel and violent. He was known for his specializations in intimidation, manipulation, thought control, and torture.

- Lieutenant General Yanagawa Heisuke was more like the stereotypical leader, and he valued discipline and liked to keep firm control over his troops.

All three of them arrived outside of Nanjing by the beginning of December. General Matsui Iwane had fallen ill by December 7th, 1937, and his replacement took over for him. As a member of the royal family, Asaka Yasuhiko had a lot more control over the men, as they would have wanted to serve him as a stand-in for the emperor. It was as if the crown had stepped in to lead them from the front lines. However, there were still two other men leading their own divisions into the city.

The commanders in Tokyo had sent the orders for the Imperial Army to occupy Nanjing on December 1st, but the men were not yet in place when the orders arrived. Matsui Iwane's health likely further delayed the plans. However, the orders were clear regardless of who was leading the troops. The Japanese had two objectives during this period:

- Take control of Beijing and establish another puppet government.

- Occupy Nanjing.

The attack on Shanghai had taken far longer than expected, so General Matsui Iwane knew how vital it was that the next major campaign did not take nearly so long to complete. With the Three Alls Policy in place, the troops had their orders to ensure that the campaign did not suffer any more delays. This was likely a contributing factor in Matsui allowing someone else to take over for the men under his command. However, before this happened, he impressed upon the men how important it was that they move swiftly and decisively. They were to represent the honor of Japan and should conduct themselves accordingly. However, it was also vital that they show how superior the Japanese were to ensure that no one else would want to face them again. He further reminded them that foreigners were to be avoided since they were not a part of the fight; they were also to "protect and patronize" any Chinese officials and citizens they encountered in the city. Matsui wanted to ensure that they avoided any misunderstandings. It is uncertain how things would have occurred if he had been the leader during the final assault on the city. It is unlikely that he would have been able to control the men enough to prevent the horrors that occurred, but he could have made an attempt to stop them. It is difficult to imagine he would have been able to prevent much of the atrocities, especially since he entered the city soon after it was captured, and the soldiers continued to inflict some of the worst treatment on civilians for over a month. They would even cease to recognize a neutral zone, inflicting the same treatment on foreigners.

Chapter 7 – Defending Against the Impossible

Before the Japanese arrived in Nanjing, the capital had an estimated population of over one million people. While the population had grown and shrunk over the centuries, since the summer of 1937, the city had seen a significant increase in the population because of the large number of Shanghai refugees. Nanjing had seemed like a safe location, but the Japanese quickly made it clear that they were going to head to the city, as it was crucial to China.

Attempted Resistance between the Cities

Soldiers who retreated from Shanghai made an effort to slow the Japanese, but they were vastly outnumbered and already tired from the fierce fighting in Shanghai. However, they attempted to stop the Japanese invaders several times during their retreat from the city.

One of the last times that the fleeing Chinese tried to stop, or at least slow, the advancing Japanese was to the east of Nanjing in the town of Kunshan. They were only able to slow the Japanese progress by a couple of days before the town fell under Japanese control. However, this did give people some time to flee, especially as the military likely would have had the occasion to tell them of the potential violence they faced when the Japanese took over Shanghai.

The soldiers managed to establish a defensive line between the cities, but the Japanese breached and destroyed it on November 19th. Seven days later, the Japanese overran the Xicheng Line. Though they had not been able to hold off the Japanese for long, it did buy the Chinese leadership more time to prepare defenses and make a strategy for how to protect Nanjing and its citizens.

The Chinese Power Struggle

One of the primary problems with Nanjing was Chinese politics and the power dynamic. There were two different thoughts on how they should defend the capital city. On one side, General Li Zongren believed that there was no point in attempting to defend the city and thought that the troops and resources were best used elsewhere. His plan was to declare the capital an open city, leaving the citizens vulnerable to an attack. Any troops in the area would be ordered to destroy resources, facilities, and goods that could be used by the Japanese. He didn't want the Imperial Army to be able to make use of the modernization that the Chinese had built up in their capital, and he was willing to completely lose the progress they had made over the decades to make it more difficult for the Japanese to move farther inland. Li Zongren thought by abandoning the city to the Japanese, Chinese troops and resources would be saved for a later confrontation when the Imperial Army would potentially be weaker. Two other important figures agreed with this plan: General Bai Chongxi and the German Army advisor, General Alexander von Falkenhausen.

However, Chiang Kai-shek was in charge of the effort, and he overruled all three of his subordinates. His concern was that simply deserting the city without even making an apparent attempt to save it would be detrimental to the nation's prestige on the international stage. He also said that such an obvious admission of their inability to fight the invaders would lower troop morale across China. He reportedly said, "I am personally in favor of defending Nanking to the death." Instead of agreeing to completely abandon the city, Chiang Kai-shek put General Tang Shengzhi in charge of 100,000 troops. The problem with the troops was that the majority of them were newly conscripted, so they were untrained. They would face Japanese forces that had recently finished a hard battle against well-trained Chinese troops in Shanghai, including a large number of elite fighters. The Chinese military personnel who were to fight for Nanjing did not stand a chance.

Tang knew that they didn't stand a chance as well, but he made a show of putting up an effort for a while. When he held a press conference on November 27th, 1937, he proudly announced that he and his men would stand and fight for China. At the same time, he warned the small population of Westerners who remained to leave because war in the city was imminent. The troops were sent to clear all of the trees and buildings within a mile of the city to prevent the Japanese from having anywhere to hide. This decision was considered very controversial, as it would mean that people fleeing from the Japanese would have to enter the city because there would be no shelter for them elsewhere. This would increase the population right before the Japanese attacked. And even if buildings were burned, they would still provide some shelter for the Japanese because the Chinese soldiers didn't have time to entirely demolish them.

Tang was fully aware that nothing he did would amount to much in the face of Japanese aggression, though. As he put on a stern front, he was attempting a couple of plans of his own. He agreed with General Li Zongren's proposition to declare Nanjing an open city. Tang seemed to put a lot of faith in the Westerners in the city because he went to them to help persuade the general that it was a mistake to fight. He also wanted them to help negotiate peace with Japan.

Though Tang tried, both plans failed, and he had to confront the Japanese with a large group of untrained men. It is unknown how many troops were active in Nanjing by the time the Japanese arrived, as some had fled prior to the invaders entering the city. However, they are thought to have outnumbered the Japanese troops.

Chapter 8– Nanjing's Disorganization and Failed Preparations

The Chinese soldiers and civilians fled Shanghai, but the Japanese soldiers were never far behind them since there was little delay between their success in Shanghai and their departure for Nanjing. The Chinese soldiers were too exhausted to put up much of a fight against the advancing soldiers, so they largely tried to slow the Japanese, with some of them surviving long enough to reach the capital city. The refugees and Chinese soldiers who headed to Nanjing found themselves again under attack by the Japanese, though it was nothing like Shanghai.

What the people in Nanjing did not know was that the military leaders knew just how hopeless the cause was. Chiang Kai-shek had made his decision to put up a front knowing that they could not win. His refusal to listen to his advisors would end up costing many of the people in the city everything.

The Questionable Preparations in Nanjing

Though the Chinese had managed to prolong the fight in Shanghai, the obvious superiority of the Japanese forces made it clear that it would be difficult to hold Nanjing.

After leaving General Tang Shengzhi in charge of Nanjing's defenses, Chiang Kai-shek sent most of the trained soldiers and government leaders from the city to set up Chongqing as a temporary capital. Chiang Kai-shek and his family left the city on December 7th to head for Chongqing.

Prior to fleeing from Nanjing, Chiang Kai-shek ordered that the citizens, including civilian government officials (only the members who were considered important to the nation), be forced to remain in the city so that they and the untrained soldiers could defend it. He went as far as to forbid the remaining soldiers from evacuating citizens. The soldiers also continued to destroy buildings, but this time inside the city.

With many of the refugees relaying the horrors of what had happened in Shanghai, many of the citizens refused to stay. Taking what they could, they left the city. However, hundreds of thousands of people remained in the city, including women, children, and elderly people. As the Japanese fighters neared, many citizens began to panic and fled the city in droves. Tang made another controversial decision and had all of the city exits closed to civilians to keep them from panicking, a decision that seems contradictory. He even burned boats that were on the Yangtze River to prevent people from leaving.

Though there were far fewer foreigners living in Nanjing than Shanghai, they did try to band together to ensure that the Japanese knew that they were a community of largely foreign businessmen and missionaries. They formed the International Committee, and they were headed by John Rabe, a German businessman. The committee worked to set up a neutral area where the Japanese and Chinese would have to refrain from fighting, and it would include a home for the civilians since they should not have been a part of the fighting. The established Safety Zone was roughly the size of Central Park (located in New York City, US), and they opened it in November 1937. Initially, they had only about a dozen refugee camps.

The Japanese arrived outside of the city on December 13th, 1937. It seems that word had already reached the people in the city that the Japanese were holding killing competitions and engaging in looting as they moved toward the city. Rumors spread that the Imperial Army was also leaving behind mass graves for those they had killed and that they were killing indiscriminately. Even though the number of Chinese soldiers was greater than the number of Japanese soldiers, their lack of substantial training and likely loss of morale (both from the desertion of their leaders and the news about the approaching army) made them a poor match for the invaders.

Comparison between Shanghai and Nanjing

If Shanghai had been a significant blow to the Japanese sense of pride, Nanjing would bolster their belief in their nation's superiority. The leadership in Shanghai had been cunning, making sure the Japanese divided their attention between different areas and forcing them to fight on several fronts. This was one of the reasons why they were able to shatter Japanese expectations that the war wouldn't take more than a few days. The Japanese had actually believed that they would be able to complete the entire war in three months, a belief that they had to reevaluate by the time they finally achieved a victory.

The Japanese military leaders were angry that they had been so wrong, and the soldiers had lost morale after the Chinese had proved that they would not be so easily defeated. However, the Japanese had faced one of the best Chinese military leaders, one who knew how to make the battle-hardy men who served him far more effective in the face of the enemy. The Imperial Army was looking for revenge and validation in their beliefs, so by the time they reached Nanjing, the soldiers were angry and ready to prove themselves. One soldier had lost his brother during the fights in the north, so when they reached Nanjing, he took out his anger about the loss by killing as many Chinese as he could. The Japanese military leaders had something particularly atrocious in mind to help harden their men, though they likely had not planned for what would happen over the first couple of months in Nanjing.

Perhaps they expected the same kind of fight that they had faced in Shanghai. It does not seem like they had any intelligence of what was happening within Nanjing beyond whatever discussions they were having with the International Committee that had created the Safety Zone. The foreigners who had established the Safety Zone had done so in a way that was similar to the one in Shanghai, so they made sure that the Japanese knew of it. The Chinese newspaper *Hankow Ta-kung-pao* had even reported on this zone, so people likely flocked to it as the Imperial Army neared. Since the leaders of the zone had let the Japanese embassy know, the embassy agreed that as long as no current or former Chinese soldiers or weapons were present, they would respect it. However, the Japanese did not provide any public support for the creation of it.

Since Tang would leave before the Japanese arrived, there was no real head of the Chinese military remaining in the city, which meant the soldiers did not stand a chance of defending it. They had months to prepare while the Second Battle of Shanghai was fought, but all of that time ended up being wasted because of the political turmoil within China. Chiang Kai-shek had no interest in protecting the city, and the remaining people in the city didn't have a strategy in how to face their enemies.

This was almost exactly what the Imperial Army had expected to face in Shanghai. And with 500,000 Imperial troops heading to the ill-prepared Nanjing, there was little that the Chinese could do.

Chapter 9 – Nanjing Falls

The attack began on December 9th, 1937, and by December 13th, the Japanese were marching into the city under the command of Prince Asaka Yasuhiko. It was the beginning of one of the worst atrocities of World War II, and the Imperial Army reveled in their quick and easy victory, especially after the difficulty they had in taking Shanghai. Over the next six weeks, the people who remained in Nanjing would face an army that was almost entirely without restraints. However, the events would not be without repercussions, as the Japanese had signed the Hague Conventions and had then gone on to ratify it. The actions of the soldiers would go directly against the agreement, and the blame for who was at fault would be one of the greatest points of contention later on.

The Retreat of the Chinese Soldiers

Japan had been sending in airstrikes against Nanjing since the beginning of December, further breaking the chain of command within the city. Outside of the city, the soldiers did not fare any better, leading to an incredibly quick defeat. With the poor coordination and lack of any real leader, the Chinese soldiers quickly realized they did not stand a chance against the invaders. Some still tried to fight, but soon, the majority of them were attempting to retreat. Knowing that they would be targeted by the invaders, many of them shed their uniforms and weapons, hoping that they would be able to blend in with the citizens.

Unfortunately, the officers had been quiet in their retreat and did not always pass on the information to their subordinates. Chinese soldiers who had not heard the order began to shoot at their own soldiers, believing that the men were deserting before the fighting even began. There were not many ways for them to retreat either, as the Japanese had nearly completely surrounded the city by that time. Some civilians also tried to flee, resulting in fewer people being able to get out of the city. After all, there was only one way for them to go, and many of them were crushed to death trying to get through the narrow gate. Some people died when they tried to climb down the walls of the city, while others drowned in the river, which was too cold for most people to swim in the winter months. The chaos going on within the city was of a very different nature than the fighting occurring outside it.

There were Japanese troops waiting along the river as well, so those who managed to get away from the city were at risk of being killed as the Japanese flotilla fired at them. Even the Chinese soldiers who made it out of the city really weren't prepared to fight the Japanese waiting outside of the walls. There was no counterattack planned.

Once it became clear that the Japanese had won, they demanded that the soldiers and citizens had to surrender or face the wrath of the Imperial Army. From a safe location outside of the city, Chiang Kai-shek refused to surrender, not wanting to look weak, especially after the events in Shanghai. Despite this refusal, he knew that the Chinese soldiers did not stand a chance, so he issued an order to the soldiers to begin evacuating the city. Unfortunately, it was too late for the people in Nanjing to leave since the Japanese were outside of the city waiting to enter.

The Hague and Geneva Conventions: Why the Citizens Should Have Been Safe

The Japanese reaction to the battle in and around Shanghai showed that they were not entirely restrained by the rules of war that had been established at the beginning of the century. However, the fact that they had been fighting in and around the city was likely used as an excuse for why their approach might have been considered justified. The Chinese fighters were fierce, giving the Japanese reason to feel that they were a real threat, even in a weakened state. Considering the ease with which the Imperial Army took Nanjing, it is possible the Chinese felt that the Imperial Army's actions wouldn't be nearly so brutal. After all, the resistance had been minimal, with most of it coming from the burning of the surrounding area prior to the Battle of Nanjing.

It is also possible that more citizens remained in the city because of the established rules around how armies were supposed to act. The expectations for how the invading army should act had been established by the Hague Conventions, which were held in 1899 and 1907 in the Netherlands. All of the world powers of the time had met to determine the way that soldiers who had been captured would be treated, as well as citizens that the military encountered. According to the agreement, it was illegal for any soldier or commander to commit war crimes. Japan was one of the nations that had signed on to the agreement, so they were bound by the established rules. The Hague Conventions even dictated the treatment of citizens and prisoners of war, prohibiting the mistreatment and killing of both groups. The Imperial Army had not followed the Hague Conventions in Shanghai, but the events leading up to their entry into Nanjing were completely different.

The Hague Conventions primarily established that anyone who was either sick or wounded would be treated by their enemies as a neutral party. The laws dictating how prisoners were to be treated were also documented in the Geneva Convention of 1929. All prisoners were to be fed and treated humanely, something that was not universally practiced up to this point. While it was generally understood by most nations that prisoners should be treated well, there was no universal law ensuring that nations and soldiers who treated prisoners poorly would be held accountable in an international court of law. It further forbade things like hostage-taking, deportations, torture, and anything that would be considered "outrages upon personal dignity," including issuing a judicial sentence against people from other nations. It was under this convention that the execution of prisoners and civilians would be explicitly designated as illegal.

However, the prevailing ideology in the Imperial Army was similar to that of the Western idea of Manifest Destiny. The Japanese believed that China was destined to fall under their control, and this was based in part because of their belief that they were superior to the people on the mainland. For those in power in Japan, it was much more practical. As an island nation, Japan heavily relied on the agriculture and resources of the mainland, and by taking control of China, the island nation would have all of the resources it needed without having to negotiate for it. Japan had managed to modernize much faster than China, and it was also united. The people in the highest echelons of the government and military planned to treat China as a colony, and they had been instilling that mindset into their soldiers, not the rules and laws that they had agreed to during the Hague Conventions. The way the Imperial Army fought in Shanghai wasn't just a result of their ferocity and the unexpected duration of the fight but was rather a result of the way the soldiers had been trained to think of their opponents. The march to Nanjing only intensified that belief as they killed and looted along the way, building up the idea that they were not only superior but invincible. It was the kind of mindset that ensured that they would ignore the conventions and enact some of the worst war crimes that the world had seen up to that point.

The City Surrounded

Though the Japanese were absolutely brutal up to this point, their actions were not illegal because the Chinese had not surrendered; they were simply fleeing. As one-sided as the fighting was, it wasn't technically illegal based on the Hague Conventions. The fact that the Japanese were an invading force likely would not have been held against them as they were following orders.

On December 12th, 1937, the Imperial Army stood outside of Nanjing, with the fighting all but over. There was no way for the Chinese soldiers or citizens to escape, and it is thought that tens of thousands of soldiers and more than 200,000 citizens were left behind to be at the mercy of the Imperial Army. The Safety Zone had a very small number of foreigners, largely Europeans and Americans, waiting to help where they could; some of the remaining people were medical professionals who hoped to help the wounded. The majority of foreigners left the city before the Japanese even arrived. There were also some Christian missionaries who remained.

On December 13th, Japan entered the city after an incredibly short fight. The Chinese citizens flocked to the Safety Zone, hoping that they would be protected in case the Imperial Army was as horrible as the rumors from Shanghai had portrayed them. They even allowed some Chinese soldiers to enter since the Japanese were so ruthless to the soldiers they encountered. One of their most important roles, though, was to serve as a neutral witness to the events that happened around them and report the atrocities back to their nations.

Commander Matsui's Commands

Though he was too sick to actually enter the city with the Imperial Army, Matsui Iwane wanted to ensure that his troops made it clear that the Japanese forces were impressive, both in terms of their abilities and their behavior. When he finally entered the city not long after the Japanese had taken over it, Matsui spoke in a way that was likely meant to be inspirational:

> I extend much sympathy to millions of innocent people in the Kiangsu and Chekiang districts, who suffered the evils of war. Now the flag of the Rising Sun is floating high over Nanking, and the Imperial Way is shining in the southern parts of the Yangtze River. The dawn of the renaissance of the East is on the verge of offering itself. On this occasion I hope for reconsideration of the situation by the 400 million people of China.

Nanjing had a long history of wars, invasions, and rebellions, but at this point in time, the city was already under a lot of strain. It had been the headquarters of the Chinese Nationalist Party. Though there was a desire to work together against the Japanese, there was also some underlying mistrust. There has been speculation that Tang Shengzhi did not have any particular loyalty to Chiang Kai-shek. This would work to Japan's advantage.

Matsui had come out of retirement to aid the military, so he would have been aware of the laws regarding citizens and prisoners, which was why he issued orders that forbade the Japanese soldiers from mistreating the Chinese people. The Imperial Army had already disobeyed this order in Shanghai, with the soldiers executing the majority of the Chinese fighters even after they had surrendered. They had also slaughtered male citizens in case those men were soldiers. They also began to steal from the surrounding area because they weren't properly supplied, particularly in regards to food. This meant that the citizens around Shanghai were left without supplies.

It is likely that Matsui hoped that his speech to the military would keep his men from enacting the same illegal behaviors in Nanjing. After all, there had been very little fighting to justify a harsh crackdown in the city. Unfortunately, the men did not listen to him.

When the Imperial Army entered the city, it was very different from their entry into Shanghai. They had only lost about one thousand soldiers, which seemed a very small price to pay in proving just how superior their army really was. They had not faced any significant fighting, and there were no big battles that actually proved their capability since the Chinese soldiers had been told to retreat before a more protracted fight could begin.

Chapter 10 – A Contest to Kill and the Execution of Chinese Prisoners of War

While the killing contest on the way to Nanjing likely is not entirely true or accurate, it did provide ideas for the Japanese soldiers. Before they had even entered the city, the Chinese soldiers in Nanjing had surrendered. According to the Hague Conventions, the soldiers who surrendered should have been taken as prisoners of war and been treated well by the Imperial Army. Instead, the Japanese soldiers would treat them as less than human.

Upon entering the city, the troops began to go through the city to round up all of the soldiers who had been unable to escape. They knew that some of the soldiers had exchanged their uniforms for civilian clothing. The Imperial Army entered homes and began to remove all men who seemed to be of draft age. The invaders even entered the Safety Zone to remove all men who could possibly be soldiers. While there were many soldiers who were rounded up, there was also a large number of men who were not affiliated with the Chinese military, including hospital employees, medical professionals, firemen, policemen, young teenagers, and others who had remained in the hopes that their lives would not be too significantly affected by the invaders. All of the men were treated as prisoners of war, regardless of if they were actually military or citizens. By December 26th, 1937, the Chinese were forced to register in the Safety Zone under the guise of ensuring that they weren't Chinese soldiers. Many of the soldiers had left the city by this time, leaving their families behind. The men between the ages of fifteen to forty-five who had remained were mostly civilians. Some of the Japanese officers had expressed the idea that it was "better ten innocents dead than an ex-soldier free," indicating just how little regard they had for their Chinese prisoners. It was also something that would help to later convict some of the Japanese officials, as this statement was completely contrary to international law.

Later, the Japanese soldiers seemed to try to make the argument that the fact that the plain-clothed soldiers were trying to hide was what made them dangerous. Considering that they had actually taken many civilians as their prisoners, not just soldiers, their argument did not hold up during the trials. Regardless of if they were soldiers or not, all of the prisoners had surrendered, meaning that they should have been treated according to the laws set forth in the Hague and Geneva Conventions.

After months of mounting resentment and a sense of superiority over the Chinese, the Japanese soldiers felt a need for vengeance against their opponents. Obviously, the need for vengeance was misplaced, as the soldiers in Nanjing had barely put up a fight. However, it was not the only reason why the Japanese took a much bleaker view of their prisoners. They had been left to largely fend for themselves, finding food where they could since the three months they spent fighting in Shanghai. Knowing that they did not even have enough food to take care of their own military and knowing that the Chinese soldiers had burned a lot of the food in the surrounding area, it did not seem possible for the invaders to properly take care of their prisoners. Not only did they not have enough food, but they also lacked sufficient space for the large number of prisoners they had taken, particularly since they failed to differentiate between soldiers and male citizens. Then there was the potential threat that the Chinese soldiers posed, at least in the minds of the Japanese men. The Chinese force was still large, and by adding civilian men into the mix, there were a lot of prisoners that they had to control. There was the risk that the prisoners might cause them difficulties, so the Japanese began to look at them as a significant problem instead of viewing them as prisoners.

The Japanese planned to hold a parade to celebrate their triumph over Nanjing, and General Matsui Iwane was to lead the men on the victory march through the city. The invading force saw the prisoners as a potential threat or perhaps as an inconvenience, as soldiers would need to stay behind to watch them. Lacking training on how to handle prisoners and with no clear policy in place for the Imperial soldiers to follow, the Japanese commanders decided to set their own policy. Instead of trying to control the prisoners, the leaders ordered the soldiers to execute all prisoners, with no effort made to determine who was actually a soldier and who was a civilian. It is unlikely that most of the orders were made orally, but there is practically no written record of them except for some remaining records issued by lower officials. One of the orders that were received and issued on December 13th stated, "Execute all the prisoners in accordance with the Brigade's order. Regarding the method for execution, what about making groups of dozens each, tying them up, and shooting them one by one."[1] There was also no expressed method in how they were to commit the executions. The soldiers began to act in ways that were decidedly contrary to the way that Matsui would have seen as acceptable; to begin with, the order itself was against the established laws of war.

---

[1] Margolin, J-L. (2006). "Japanese Crimes in Nanjing, 1937-1938: A Reappraisal," *China Perspectives*, January/February 2006.

As a result, soldiers took it upon themselves to act in ways that were far crueler than simple executions. Perhaps inspired by the idea of the killing competition that they had discussed on the way to Nanjing, members of the Imperial Army began to follow through with the orders in whatever way they considered appropriate or entertaining. Some simply lined up their prisoners and executed them, similar to a firing squad. Others took to using their bayonets for a much more up-close and personal execution of their helpless prisoners. Some seemed to try to follow through with the idea of a competition, lining up between one hundred and two hundred men along the banks of the Yangtze River and then gunning them down with machine guns. Perhaps the most gruesome and cruel method of execution was conducted by the officers who had swords. These officers, who were supposed to control their own men, seemed more interested in showing just how brutal they could be, forcing prisoners to kneel before them before beheading them. There were reports of competitions among many of the soldiers to see who could kill the most prisoners, particularly as they tried to gun down as many as possible during one frenzied attack on the Chinese soldiers. Beheading was one of the most popular methods of brutal execution, but some Japanese soldiers used even more drastic and barbaric methods, including nailing their prisoners to trees, burning them alive, and hanging the prisoners by their tongues.

Many of the horrors that were conducted against the prisoners were actually captured by reporters and photographers. The documentation and images of the massacre of the defeated soldiers are still available, with some posted online as a reminder of just how horrific the experience was almost as soon as the Japanese soldiers arrived in the city (these images are difficult to look at due to the brutality depicted in them, so they have not been included in this book). It is likely that the soldiers did not know that their actions were illegal, but as the images show, what they did was clearly wrong. In the years following the end of World War II, soldiers would say that they were simply following the orders given to them. Some may have felt that their method of execution was acceptable because of how savagely the officers had attacked. The way they would recount the events of that first week is haunting, particularly as it was so similar to how soldiers in Nazi Germany were willing to follow their equally horrific orders.

By the end of that first week, an estimated forty thousand Chinese men had been murdered by the invaders. It was the first major war crime that would be committed over the course of World War II. Unfortunately, it was just the beginning of the horrors following the surrender of the city. The slaughter of soldiers and men who were at an age to be drafted was the start of a nightmare for the civilians who remained within the city. While the majority of the Chinese men were slaughtered in the first few days, those who were still alive would largely be killed before the Japanese commanders would regain control over their men.

Chapter 11 – The Rape of Tens of Thousands of People

As the Chinese prisoners were being executed outside of the city, the Japanese soldiers who remained inside the city walls began to commit atrocities against the citizens. Unlike the soldiers acting on orders outside of the city, the men who had entered Nanjing had no such orders to cause harm. Their actions would come to be classified as criminal acts, which means that the actions of these soldiers were not done in any military capacity. The soldiers have been said to have been undisciplined, but based on the barbarity of the attacks against unarmed citizens, the problem was not based on the soldiers' lack of discipline but indicated a much deeper problem.

The next three chapters examine the three primary types of crimes that the Japanese committed against the Chinese citizens who had no means of escaping Nanjing.

The first type of crime would come to be the inspiration for one of the names of the Nanjing Massacre: the Rape of Nanjing. For six weeks, the male Japanese soldiers moved around the city, doing whatever they pleased. A large number of them began to hunt women. They did not care how old a female was, with the age range for women and girls who were assaulted being between ten and sixty. The youngest known victim was only nine years old, while the oldest was in her seventies. Pregnant women were not safe either. Women were abducted and then raped by individuals or gang-raped by groups of soldiers who did not view them as people.

After being raped, many of the women were mutilated and killed, with children also falling victim to the barbaric actions of the invaders. Young children and infants who were considered in the way of soldiers who wanted to attack and rape their mothers or sisters were killed. Mothers and grandmothers who tried to prevent their younger generations from being taken were also killed.

While there were times when individual soldiers would act to rape women, more often than not, the invaders acted in small groups so that a woman would be assaulted repeatedly at one time and would likely face the same torture at a later date if they weren't brutally mutilated and killed after being gang-raped. These soldiers would eventually have to talk about what they had done, and they would say that they didn't want to kill the women after raping them but that they couldn't leave behind any evidence. During the war tribunals, soldiers generally had an easier time recounting the looting and killing they had committed, but they were visibly uncomfortable talking about what they had done to the women before killing them.

Women were raped in front of each other, and at times, they were raped in front of their families. Some of the women who were abducted were taken to where the Japanese soldiers lodged and would be held overnight or, in some cases, for more than a week, where they would be repeatedly assaulted as soldiers came and went. Those who were kept for longer periods of time were often forced to work for the soldiers, serving them and cleaning during the day, then being sexual slaves at night.

Women who resisted were attacked, often with the soldiers wielding bayonets. Sometimes resistance meant that their families would be attacked. Not all the women were murdered, likely because the soldiers knew that they would not have any further outlets for their urges if they killed all of them. It would take a while for a place to be established for comfort women, in large part because Nanjing would need to be safe before these women could be brought in. Since there wouldn't be an official establishment for those services, the women of Nanjing were sometimes forced into that position.

Over time, the Japanese soldiers even began to enter the designated Safety Zone to find women who had not already been raped and assaulted. The German leader, John Rabe, had one of the only effective ways to force the Japanese out of the zone without giving them a reason to attack. As the person in control of the Safety Zone, Rabe could stop them by showing the invaders his Nazi armband with the familiar swastika. The Japanese may have felt that they were superior to the Chinese, and it is quite likely that many of them felt that they were superior even to their allies, but the soldiers were not willing to risk getting into trouble for disobeying an easily recognizable ally. Even if the Japanese had not officially recognized the Safety Zone, a Nazi was in charge of the area, and he was clearly taking the role very seriously. Over the weeks of chaos, Rabe ended up taking up a position of protector, going around in his vehicle to help people in the Safety Zone from being assaulted. There are several stories of how he drove away soldiers who were raping women, once throwing a soldier off of a woman. There was another time when he startled another soldier so much that the man ran away without putting his pants on. His presence seemed to have caused the Japanese soldiers to fear being caught, a sentiment that the soldiers did not have for their own officers. This is an unfortunate illustration of how little the officers did to stop their own men. Other people in the zone would not have as much success in preventing the rape of Chinese citizens who were looking for refuge. This shows that there was a complete lack of respect for foreign nations, especially as people from within the Safety Zone began to send reports of Japanese behavior after they entered the city.

The raping, mutilation, and murder of women would last for much longer than the slaughter of the soldiers. Where most of the soldiers and young men were killed within a week, the women would be victimized for the six weeks the Japanese rampaged through Nanjing. It has been estimated that between 10 and 30 percent of women between the ages of fifteen and forty became sexual assault victims during this time. Some reports indicated that at the worst of the chaos, the soldiers were raping up to one thousand women a night. According to the Westerners who had stayed in the Safety Zone, they witnessed between eight thousand and twenty thousand incidents of rape, and there is no way to tell how many sexual assaults were actually perpetrated since there were no witnesses at times to report them.

The number of women who were raped is impossible to know because the soldiers did not keep records of this particular atrocity. There doesn't seem to have been any particular orders to address the problem either, with soldiers seeming to have been allowed to do as they pleased during the six weeks after they entered the city. However, there were witnesses to the barbaric treatment of the women, and it would mentally scar those who lived through the chaos.

Chapter 12 – Mass Killings and Desecration of the Dead

Almost as if to mirror the executions occurring outside of the city, the Japanese soldiers within the city seemed to want to relieve their aggressions in a similar way. They began to randomly stab citizens—women, children, and the elderly—with bayonets without warning. Some began to viciously attack and mutilate the citizens with knives, and the invaders seemed to be unconcerned as they ran over citizens with tanks as they made their way through the city.

Regular citizens were shot down in the streets when they tried to flee from angry soldiers. People who refused to give the Japanese what they wanted were killed. Reverend John Magee said of the invading soldiers that they "not only killed every prisoner they could find but also a vast number of ordinary citizens of all age[s]. Many of them were shot down like the hunting of rabbits in the streets. There are bodies all over the city." Some have described these killings as indiscriminate murders. While less was done to investigate the raping of women, the random slaughter of citizens was investigated almost immediately after order was restored to the city.

Over a six-week period, there were reports that some officers encouraged their men to be more inventive in how they killed the citizens. After several weeks of mindlessly killing many of the city's residents, bodies lay all over the city, and the roads were mixed with bodily fluids, precipitation, and fuel. The Japanese were aware that this was an ideal condition for numerous illnesses to fester, so they were forced to change how they continued to kill the people of Nanjing.

It seemed that all pretext of pretending to be concerned about soldiers was gone, and the Imperial soldiers began to round up citizens to kill them in locations that have since been described as slaughter pits. Whether or not they were actually directed to do so, the soldiers did start to become more creative and crueler in their methods of killing the people at their mercy. Some of the civilians were buried alive, while others became living practice dummies for soldiers, who practiced maneuvers with swords and bayonets. Other innocent civilians were covered in gasoline and burned alive, something that had been done to Chinese soldiers during the first week. The location where these unimaginably inhumane acts occurred was near the Yangtze River, so the soldiers threw their victims in the water to be taken from the city when they were done. Some have described the river as being so full of human bodies that it appeared to be red with their blood.

Initially, the Japanese seemed to try to properly take care of the bodies following the killings. Between December 24th,1937, and January 6th, 1938, over 5,700 bodies were buried near the Hepingmen Gate, including both soldiers and civilians. Between January 6th and May 31st, 1938, nearly seven thousand bodies were buried elsewhere. The Japanese recorded that roughly fifty-seven thousand people were buried, but they did not have the manpower and money to continue to bury all of their victims. After some sort of order was restored, residents from the city would begin to bury some of the dead, and it is estimated that 260,000 were buried by the end. But not all the bodies were buried. Some were burned, others were left in the river, and others were used for target practice. The bodies of the victims were often treated with as little respect as the living Chinese civilians.

There is no record of just how many people were killed during this time. However, the body count should not be the focus of the atrocities; instead, what is important is the undeniable evidence of a large-scale massacre. Whole numbers can be debated, but there is simply too much evidence to ignore that war crimes had been committed by the Japanese. The methods of killing the Chinese outside the city showed that at least the execution of the prisoners of war was not a result of undisciplined soldiers doing whatever they wanted but of a complete disregard of international law by the officers. The executions were systematic and well organized, even if the methods were not uniform. There is little evidence of direct orders for most of the killings that occurred within the city, but with the raping and killing of civilians going on for weeks, it is impossible to ignore that the officials at least tolerated the behavior. All of this was clear to those who witnessed what was happening, and it would come back against the officers and those in command after the end of the war. Until that time, though, the leaders did little to bring their officers under control until the Japanese high command finally learned of the events and sent orders to stop the chaos within the city. Whatever the military leaders in Japan wanted, the massacre of the Chinese civilians certainly was not a part of their plan. They ultimately wanted to control China, which meant that they needed a workforce and buildings from which to rule.

For a month and a half, the city was a living nightmare for the people who resided there, and even after order was restored, they would have little hope that the Japanese would honor international law; after all, both the Chinese and the Westerners had seen how little the Japanese military and government controlled their invading force.

Chapter 13 – Stealing the Valuables and Destroying the City

As the Japanese soldiers made their way through the city, they began to steal from the citizens, often at gunpoint. Soon, they began entering homes, stealing what they could take with them when they left the city. As if trying to hide what they had done, they began to burn buildings and homes. They also vandalized Nanjing, further destroying the city after the bombings that had occurred prior to the Imperial Army's arrival.

During the chaotic reign of the soldiers, extensive looting and arson took place around the city, similar to what the Nazis would do in Jewish ghettos a few years later. The primary difference was that the Japanese were destroying older buildings, stores, and homes in a city with historical significance to the Chinese. This could have been a method to further demoralize the Chinese living in other cities.

While the soldiers did not destroy the buildings within the Safety Zone, they did steal from the refugees who were there. The invaders took food and what little possessions that the refugees had. There wasn't much the International Committee in the Safety Zone could do to stop the soldiers from what they did outside of the zone, and there were only a few actions they could take against soldiers in the Safety Zone, as the soldiers could turn against them as well. Given the horrors that the soldiers were committing around them, it is easy to see the dilemma that the International Committee and the Westerners faced. To keep any kind of protection for refugees, they couldn't do much of anything to intervene in what they were witnessing. Fortunately, many of the vital facilities were located within the Safety Zone, including medical facilities, administrative buildings, and educational buildings. This did mean that most of the structures that housed things of monetary value (such as art) were vulnerable to the soldiers.

Some of the looting was chaotic, but there were elements of it that were far more calculated and efficient. Trucks were brought in to take away larger objects, creating something akin to a convoy. These trucks quickly removed valuables from Nanjing, probably to ensure that the things didn't burn when they could help fund the army. This particular crime was not perpetrated only by the soldiers, as the officials also participated as well. The officers often had the first pick of what they wanted and looted the most valuable items. One of the more notorious officers, Lieutenant General Nakajima Kesago, responded to General Matsui Iwane (who was upset by the looting) by saying, "Why does the stealing of art pieces matter so much when we are stealing a country and human lives? Who would benefit from these items even if we left them behind?" As callous as this sounds, the lieutenant general did have a point. Matsui had failed to stop other crimes that were far worse; the theft of items was not nearly so important.

When most of the valuables were gone, the Japanese began to destroy the buildings that remained standing. The only area that seemed to be largely left alone was the Safety Zone. Nearly every other part of the city would be all but unlivable by the end of those first six weeks. It is estimated that as much as a third of Nanjing was demolished by looting and other acts of destruction. Shops and businesses were completely looted, so there would not be much for the Chinese to return to once something like normalcy was restored in Nanjing.

How much of this was ordered by Japanese officials is difficult to say, but it is obvious that they knew what the soldiers were doing around the city. The number of burning buildings without any active fighting would have been impossible to miss. It was probably permitted (if it wasn't ordered) because it would help to destroy Chinese culture within the city. With the deterioration of the ancient culture, it would be easier for the Japanese to come into the city and reshape it as they pleased. The Japanese did spend most of 1937 and 1938 trying to divide China into fragments that would be easier to control. It was only after facing a lot of resistance that the Japanese would stop trying to break up the nation (during 1939 and 1940) and simply strive to conquer the nation as it was.

Chapter 14 – Reports of the Rapes and Atrocities Reach the Generals and Investigations Begin

One of the greatest debates that have occurred since the horrific events in Nanjing was determining who was to blame and how high up the chain of command one needed to go to find the culprits.

The Accounting of the Events from the Nanjing Safety Zone

Though the Imperial Army did not entirely honor the Nanjing Safety Zone, many of the foreigners who lived there were left alone (although the Chinese citizens were not as lucky). The Safety Zone acted as a place of refuge for as many as 200,000 Chinese citizens, and the foreigners took in as many people as they could between the arrival of the Japanese and until the zone was dissolved in February.

The foreigners soon acted in an equally critical role when the Japanese soldiers began raping and killing citizens, something that they knew was against the laws of war established by the Hague Conventions.

Initially, the European and American citizens began to send reports to Japanese diplomats, hoping that they would intercede and stop the barbaric practices of their own soldiers. These letters include accounts of the things that the Westerners in the Safety Zone witnessed, which they had added to emphasize that the presence of foreigners was not enough to persuade the soldiers to act in accordance with the laws. The letters came to be known as the "Cases of Disorder," a name that doesn't accurately reflect the severity of the problems or the contents of those letters. As a result of the horrors, the International Committee within the Safety Zone began to record the events, perhaps in case the Japanese did not do anything to stop the raping and unchecked massacres or perhaps so that they could report back to their own nations to let them know how brutal the Japanese soldiers were. It is also possible that the people within the Safety Zone planned to use the information against the Japanese later on as proof that war crimes had been committed. One of the recorded accounts from the Cases of Disorder recalled some of the actions of the Japanese soldiers at a Chinese temple:

> Many Japanese soldiers arrived, round[ed] up all the young women, chose 10, and raped them in a room at the temple. Later the same day a very drunken Japanese soldier came into one room demanding wine and women. Wine was given, but no girls. Enraged, he started to shoot wildly, killing two young boys, then left.

This is just one of many harrowing accounts of how little regard the Japanese soldiers had for the people living within the city. Another Westerner who wrote home about what had happened was Robert Wilson. He recounted the events he had witnessed, although it is uncertain why he would retell the events to his family as they were fairly traumatic.

> The slaughter of civilians is appalling. I could go on for pages telling of cases of rape and brutality almost beyond belief. Two bayoneted cases are the only survivors of seven street cleaners who were sitting in their headquarters when Japanese soldiers came in without warning or reason and killed five of their number and wounded the two that found their way to the hospital.

- December 15, Robert Wilson

> They [Japanese soldiers] bayoneted one little boy, killing him, and I spent an hour and a half this morning patching up another little boy of eight who had five bayonet wounds including one that penetrated his stomach, a portion of omentum was outside the abdomen

- December 19, Robert Wilson

Accounts like these recorded by the International Committee would later be used to help highlight just how out of control the invaders were in those early days and how slow the Japanese government and commanders were to bring the problem under control.

Ultimately, it was the letters and cases that the Westerners kept during those nightmarish six weeks that would become the record of what had happened. Many of these documents are still available. There are far fewer accounts from the victims themselves, though they likely had no one to ask for help. The officials had fled before the invaders had even arrived, leaving behind largely untrained soldiers and citizens to fend for themselves against an incredibly hostile and agitated enemy. Still, there are some accounts of what happened from the Chinese victims, and they are kept with the accounts written by the Westerners.

In another strange twist of irony, John Rabe wrote to Adolf Hitler, hoping that the Führer would intervene to save the Chinese citizens. It is a strange note of sympathy by a person who was a part of a party that would enact equally horrific atrocities in Europe. Both sides seemed able to recognize the atrocities of the other while failing to correlate the same condemnation for their own. It gave both sides a sense of superiority over the other while having the same inability to recognize how similar their ideologies were. Whatever was said in Rabe's pleas, Hitler chose to ignore the appeal for help. Along with his requests for help, Rabe kept his own diary of the events. This would eventually be made available for people to read at the end of the century, showing just what the people in the city experienced as the Japanese soldiers moved about unchecked and uncontrolled around the city.

The High Command's Reaction

As of February 5th, 1938, members of the International Committee had sent over 450 correspondences to the Japanese Embassy alone, detailing the behavior of the invading soldiers. Many of the activities of the soldiers within the city had not been committed based on orders from the Japanese high command, so the accounts from the Westerners were likely shocking. In addition, the reports were too numerous to ignore. Japan's military had tight control over the media narratives about what the troops were doing, and the events in Nanjing were definitely something they did not want the Japanese people to learn about, so they went to great lengths to cover up any records of what had happened, starting with the reports that were taken by those in the city.

Knowing full well just what kinds of atrocities their soldiers had committed in Nanjing, the military continued to portray the men as heroes so that the general Japanese population would continue to support the nation's drive to become an empire. They seemed to be following the traditional method used by every other nation that strove to be an empire, regardless of how successful those nations were in the long run.

The First Investigation Begins

In March 1938, an investigation into this obvious criminal activity began. It was headed by Lewis Smythe, an American Christian missionary and sociologist who had remained in the Safety Zone. With the assistance of approximately twenty students from Nanjing University, they began to collect data about the number of people killed during those chaotic weeks following Japan's victory.

They first went to Jiangning Xian, which was located outside of Nanjing, where they obtained some staggering statistics.

- Roughly 9,160 people were murdered in the region.

- Over three-quarters of those killed were men.

- Nearly 60 percent of the murdered male civilians were men between the ages of fifteen and forty-four, and they were likely killed under the guise of ensuring that they weren't soldiers.

- About 11 percent of the women killed were between fifteen and forty-four years old. This age group was also the most targeted for rape.

- About 83 percent of the women killed were over forty-five years old.

- Roughly 8 percent of those who were killed were children between the ages of five and fourteen, and about 2 percent were children who were four years old and younger.

These findings suggested that more older women remained behind, likely believing that they would be somewhat respected by the Imperial Army. These women probably were tasked with ensuring that their homes and stores were protected and that order would be restored as soon as possible. The rest of their families had either fled from the area or, especially if the Japanese were too close, headed to the Safety Zone. This would explain why there were fewer people in the region but a higher number of elderly women. Due to the number of older women killed, it is clear that the Japanese did not provide them any amount of respect. Some of the women were killed outright, while others were left in the buildings when the soldiers burned them to the ground.

Chapter 15 – Declaring the Restoration of Order

Ironically, the Japanese had started trying to get Chinese citizens to return to work during the early part of January 1938, even as the soldiers continued to rape, loot, and kill them. One of the reasons this was necessary was that the Japanese simply did not have the necessary supplies to feed themselves. They had managed to make off with a lot of valuables, but those objects wouldn't be worth anything if the Japanese did not survive the occupation of Nanjing. By the end of January, the Japanese soldiers had started forcing people who had taken refuge in the Safety Zone to return to their homes or whatever remained of their homes.

When alone with one of his assistants, General Matsui Iwane was said to have expressed his shock at how horribly out of control things had gotten:

> I now realize that we have unknowingly wrought a most grievous effect on this city. When I think of the feelings and sentiments of many of my Chinese friends who have fled from Nanjing and of the future of the two countries, I cannot but feel depressed. I am very lonely and can never get in a mood to rejoice about this victory...I personally

feel sorry for the tragedies to the people, but the Army must continue unless China repents. Now, in the winter, the season gives time to reflect. I offer my sympathy, with deep emotion, to a million innocent people.

- General Matsui (reported in Iris Chang's *The Rape of Nanking: The Forgotten Holocaust*, 1991)

General Matsui was aware of what was happening in the city, and several times, he issued orders to his men to "behave properly," something he had originally instructed them to do. However, these were not the kinds of well-trained soldiers that he had become accustomed to. The soldiers were younger and had been trained under a different ideology than what had been prevalent when General Matsui had initially served in the military. It is said that when he stood to address the Imperial Army in February 1938, he was holding back tears. As he upbraided the men who had behaved in a way that was contrary to what was honorable, he believed that the actions in Nanjing would do irreparable damage to the image that the Japanese military had tried to create. Perhaps he knew that there were simply too many witnesses for the crimes to be completely covered up. From the Westerners who had been there to witness it to the living victims, Matsui probably had enough experience in war to know that the damage done was on too large a scale for it to be swept under the rug. It was also likely that he was ashamed that he had not kept his men under control. Compared to the other two commanders and the prince, General Matsui had built his reputation on honor and respect. Nothing about what happened since the army arrived in China had met his expectations of how the Chinese should have been treated. It is also likely that he knew that Western nations would focus more on the events in Nanjing and find it to be proof that the Japanese had become modern only in regards to their economy. The actions of the military were barbaric and chaotic, something that would definitely taint Japan's reputation around the world.

The Safety Zone was dissolved in February 1938 as the Japanese began to establish a government for the city. As Japan tried to create some semblance of order, they began to recall the people who were responsible for keeping the men under control. Matsui and Prince Asaka Yasuhiko were both told to return to Japan, where General Matsui resumed his retirement from active military service. It is thought that he may have suffered from tuberculosis, and he had also shown that he was no longer able to keep control over men the way he had when he was younger. Though he was retired, the former general did act as a military advisor for the next two years, helping the Cabinet as they made decisions on how to proceed as they fought farther into China and began heading south toward the Philippines. In the early part of 1940, Matsui was actively helping to get a statue of Kannon (the Japanese deity of mercy and pets) made and placed in Atami, the town where he lived. When it was erected, the statue was turned to face the direction of Nanjing. Later in the war, he did travel some, going to Burma, China, Malaya, Thailand, and a few other places in his role as the president of the Greater Asia Association. For most of the rest of World War II, his role was more muted, though the former general did remain active over most of the time between 1938 and 1945.

Chapter 16 – Wang Ching-wei, the Puppet Government, and the End of the War

The upper echelons of the Japanese military and government knew that they needed to put someone in charge of the city who would help to quell the unrest that their soldiers had caused. Clearly, they could not put a Japanese citizen as the head of the Chinese city, so they found someone they felt they could control. The man they selected was Wang Ching-wei. By the time Wang died, the Japanese had much more significant problems, so the region was largely left to fend for itself.

A Brief History of Wang Ching-wei

Born in 1883, Wang had been raised as a student of traditional Chinese education. His family was a part of the minor gentry in China at a time when there was much political upheaval. He learned all of the important cultural arts, including calligraphy, poetry, and Chinese prose. This would help him become an adept orator as he grew up. He first seemed to take an interest in the government in 1903 when he successfully took the civil service exam. This earned him a scholarship that would take him to Japan, where he attended Tokyo Law College. During his time in Japan, he would become one of the founding members of the T'ung Meng Hui, an association that sought a revolution in China. Due to his amazing way with words, he became one of the major propagandists for the group. Wang gained attention as a national figure when he helped in the attempted assassination of the Chinese prince regent. When that failed, Wang was arrested for his role and was jailed between 1910 and 1911. During the 1911 Revolution, he became one of the primary negotiators between the two sides.

Wang married in 1912, then moved to France, where he continued his education until 1917. Upon his return to China, he resumed actively supporting Sun Yat-sen, the first president of the Republic of China. During this time, Wang distinguished himself, and that when Sun died in 1925, Wang became the head of the KMT (the Kuomintang Party) and the revolutionary government that they were forming. When Chiang Kai-shek led a military coup against the revolutionaries in 1926, Wang fled from the region. He would return the following year, soon becoming the leader of the Nationalists' Wuhan government. Initially, he and his party aligned with Chiang, but within a year, Wang found himself disagreeing with the Communists. As his views changed, the party forced Wang out of the leadership position that he had held in the party. He found a new position as the primary opponent of Chiang and his methods within the KMT, and he supported several attempts to oust Chiang from power until 1932.

Following the Manchurian Incident (when Japan managed to reoccupy the region in 1931), Wang and Chiang put aside their differences as they realized that there was a much bigger problem they had to face. The pair formed a coalition and worked to establish a policy of minimal resistance as the Japanese took over the region. Both Wang and Chiang knew that the Chinese military was not strong enough to face the Japanese, so they were hoping to buy some time to build and strengthen the army. Between 1931 and 1935, Wang served as the prime minister, working with his opponent until there was an assassination attempt on his life. The attempt was unsuccessful, but Wang was hurt, and the bullet remained in his body. Perhaps feeling that he was no longer able to serve in the capacity they needed, the party and Chiang forced Wang to retire.

As the Second Sino-Japanese War began, Chiang's control over the party would increase, while Wang's power would continually be diminished. Wang's forced retirement did not stop him from participating in politics and the party, and he was able to get another high position within the KMT. However, he became more of a symbol than a member with actual power. As he was no longer instrumental in the power dynamic, Wang would have a better vantage point to see how the Chinese were suffering under Chiang, as well as to hear rumors of how the Japanese were treating the Chinese people during 1937. It was said that he acted in a way that he thought would ease the suffering of the Chinese people, as well as in a way that was designed to weaken Chiang's power over the party. Wang wanted to establish a peace settlement with the Japanese to stop the violence.

Following the Rape of Nanjing and the other atrocities committed by the Japanese forces as they moved farther into China, Wang's ideas would be unacceptable. During December 1938, he would be forced to flee from China, finally settling temporarily in Hanoi. Since he had been trying to work with the Japanese prior to his departure from China, they decided to offer him a position to head a new regime in China. The Japanese leaders assured him that he would be autonomous, so Wang accepted the position.

Japan Loses Control as Germany Falls

Despite the assurances that he would be in control, Wang was little more than a puppet for the Japanese government. He was also very ineffective in his attempts to stop the fighting in his region. Wang held his position until 1944. That year, Wang tried to have the bullet removed from his body, and during the operation, he died, leaving the region with no puppet for the Japanese to control. However, by this point, the US had entered World War II. The young nation, angry about the attack on Pearl Harbor, was proving to require nearly all of the attention of the Imperial Army. Trying to control the regions of China was not as important as stopping the US from attacking Japan.

No matter how hard the Japanese fought, they had no path forward to win. They were stretched too thin and were trying to control regions where the Chinese had executed scorched earth policies, so they simply did not have access to the resources they needed to stand up to the US. They also could not rely on Germany. Hitler and his nation were clearly not going to win their fight in Europe. On May 8th, 1945, Germany unconditionally surrendered to the Allies. While most of Europe was destroyed by the war, the US had joined World War II late (they declared war on the Axis Powers in December 1941, following the Japanese attack on Pearl Harbor, Hawaii). Apart from the attack at Pearl Harbor, very little of the US had been affected by the war (Germany and Japan had tried to attack with balloons and submarines, but by 1945, both nations were too focused on protecting their own lands). The US was rich in resources, had a much larger population, and its military forces had not spent nearly so many years fighting. Japan had started the Second Sino-Japanese War in the summer of 1937, which means they had been fighting for over four years by the time the US joined. By 1945, the Japanese had been fighting for nearly a decade, while the US had only been engaged for four years.

In addition to having more resources and less weary soldiers, the US had something that the rest of the world did not know about: the first nuclear weapons. It was clear at the beginning of 1945 that Germany would soon fall, so British Prime Minister Winston Churchill, US President Franklin Delano Roosevelt, and Soviet Premier Joseph Stalin met in Yalta to discuss what to do with Germany and how to end the war in Asia. At the time, the US wasn't sure when the nuclear weapons would be functional, so when the group met in Yalta (in what's come to be known as the Yalta Conference) in February 1945, the UK and the US saw value in having the land support of the Soviet Union. The three national leaders discussed how the Soviets would attack Japan, even though Japan and the Soviet Union had established a peace agreement a few years earlier. If the Soviets provided military support against Japan, they would be given a lot of influence over Manchuria following the Japanese surrender. They also decided how they would divide up the nations that the Nazis had invaded, with the Soviets gaining a lot of influence over the eastern part of Europe and the UK and the US having more influence over the western part.

Roosevelt died soon thereafter, and Vice President Harry Truman became the president. The hope that the US and the USSR would be able to take a less adversarial role following the war was soon quashed, for Truman's administration conflicted with the Soviet leader. When Churchill was voted out of office and a new prime minister joined the three nations, Stalin was said to have refused to even recognize the new leader. The combative relationship between the countries became much more pronounced after Germany surrendered. Stalin still held up his end of the agreement, though, sending his men over to fight Japan. The US worked as quickly as possible to finish the bombs in the hope that they could force the Japanese to surrender before the Soviets engaged in fighting. If the Japanese surrendered first, the agreement from the Yalta Conference would not be valid, so the Soviets would not have as much say.

In addition to wanting to nullify the agreement with the Soviet Union, the US was also concerned with the number of lives that would be lost if the fighting continued. The Japanese were much stronger than the Germans were by 1945 (they did not face the same level of resistance that the Germans did), so estimates said that the war would go on for years. The atrocities that the Japanese had carried out in the regions that they controlled were fairly well known, so the loss of life would likely have been much greater. However, the US focused mostly on the loss of their own soldiers in their calculations. Ultimately, they decided if the atomic weapons could end the war faster, it was worth the loss of Japanese civilian lives.

In the early part of August 1945, the US dropped leaflets over several Japanese cities (a common practice used during World War II), warning the citizens that they were going to be bombed. This not only acted as a way to reduce morale, but it also pushed the citizens to pressure their government to surrender. In theory, it also gave them time to flee. This initial set of warning leaflets was called the "LeMay leaflets," and they were dropped over Hiroshima. The warning was pretty standard; however, there was no mention of a new bomb that would be worse than anything the people could imagine at the time. The second round of leaflets was dropped over several other cities, and the image included a mushroom cloud. However, the text discussed the coming Soviet invasion, which would start on August 9th, 1945. Records suggest that Nagasaki did not receive this leaflet until after the city had been almost completely destroyed.

As they warned the people, the US, the UK, and the USSR warned Japan to surrender before the end of July, something that Japan refused to do. Perhaps the Japanese could not yet recognize that their defeat was imminent, even without the use of nuclear weapons. However, they were the last remaining Axis Power, which means that all of their enemies were entirely focused on them. It wasn't a question of if but when they would lose.

On August 6th, 1945, just before 9 a.m. in Japan, a small group of US bombers flew over Hiroshima. All of them released bombs so that the pilot and crew would suffer from the same amount of guilt after the destruction of the city. The Americans may not have known exactly how destructive it would be, but they did anticipate that it would be worse than any of the previous aerial bombings. Later, it would become known that the crew of the *Enola Gay* was the aircraft that carried the live nuclear weapon nicknamed "Little Boy." The crew would later express pride in their efforts, not grief or guilt, something that seems more chilling now since the effects of the bomb have become well known.

The Japanese suddenly lost all contact with an entire city. They were again warned to surrender, but the military leaders were attempting to figure out what had happened. The US only gave them three days, which was not enough time for them to witness the devastation—it wasn't enough time for the Japanese to fully consider their options, as atomic weaponry was beyond most people's comprehension at the time.

On August 9th, 1945, just after 11 a.m. in Japan, the US dropped its second atomic weapon on the city of Nagasaki. One survivor, Reiko Hada, who was only nine years old at the time of the bombing, relived the experience:

> A blazing light shot across my eyes. The colors were yellow, khaki, and orange, all mixed together. I didn't even have time to wonder what it was...In no time, everything went completely white. It felt as if I had been left all alone. The next moment there was a loud roar. Then I blacked out.

Japan gave its unconditional surrender on August 14th, 1945. The final surrender was signed on September 2nd, 1945. World War II was over, but the Cold War was about to start. The adversarial relationship between the US and Japan would quickly change as the relationship between the US and the USSR became more tense. The

US knew it needed more allies in the East to prevent the further spread of communism in Asia.

With the end of World War II, the Chinese Civil War would resume, but whichever side won, the nation would be communist. That left just a few nations as potential allies for the US, including Japan. Unlike the nations in the West, where power and influence were largely divided between the UK, the USSR, France, and the US, Japan was under the near-complete control of the US (the regions Japan had occupied were restored to their respective countries, except for Manchuria, which was under the influence of the USSR because of the Yalta Conference). This quick shift in perceived enemies would cause problems in holding the Japanese accountable for what they had done. However, the stories of the horrors of the Japanese occupation across Asia would not go completely unpunished. There had been too many witnesses to what had happened in Nanjing for the Japanese military to go entirely free.

Following the Japanese surrender, American troops were sent to Nanjing to restore order as quickly and as safely as possible. They arrived on September 3rd, 1945. The entire airfield where they landed was under Japanese control. With about fifty Americans and less than three hundred Chinese citizens, they were vastly outnumbered by the seventy thousand Japanese soldiers. These Japanese soldiers had not seen the devastation in their own country, so they were displeased with the orders to lay down their weapons. Still, they would not disobey orders, so the city was fairly quickly occupied by the US. Nanjing was far more organized than Shanghai, which was said to be in chaos following the end of the war. Both cities would soon fall under the control of the Chinese government and the leader of one of the two factions, Mao Zedong. By 1950, most of the foreigners had left Nanjing.

Chapter 17 – The Nanjing War Crimes Tribunal and John Rabe's Life after the Events in Nanjing

As the world looked for answers to how things could have gotten so out of control to result in a second world war, with both Germany and Japan committing some of the worst atrocities in modern memory, the victorious nations began to look to hold people accountable. Just like the Nuremberg trials that sought to hold the German commanders accountable for the Holocaust and other war crimes, the Allies started to put prominent Japanese government officials and military commanders on trial. The events at Nanjing were some of the worst war crimes that the Japanese would be held accountable for after the war ended.

Documentation of the Atrocities

The Westerners in the Safety Zone had documented what they had witnessed during those six weeks in December 1937 and January 1938, with letters, diaries, and pleas to outside nations to intercede. These would again be brought forth, but they were not the only recorded details about that nightmarish time. As mentioned, the Japanese had embedded reporters, as well as the military, who kept their own records. Perhaps the most disturbing part of the records that the Japanese kept were the haunting photographs that showed men standing over their helpless victims as they prepared to execute men who were clearly unarmed. Soldiers posed while holding swords over their victims, whose eyes were usually downcast as they knew what was coming. There are many pictures of the horrific killings, but they did not record the rapes, perhaps knowing just how those photos would be perceived.

These pictures showed a side of the soldiers that would be deemed base instead of glorious. Some Chinese citizens actually got their hands on some of the pictures or the negatives. After making duplicate copies, they then snuck the pictures out of China. This undermined the attempts by the Japanese high command to destroy all of the evidence of what had occurred in the city. As the victorious nations began to prepare to start a trial, the pictures were provided as proof of wrongdoing. These harrowing images would be strong evidence against all levels of the Japanese military because officers and other officials could be easily recognized watching and participating in the war crimes.

Japanese soldiers and officers would eventually speak about what had happened. Some admitted what they had done during the tribunal, while others had kept diaries that were not destroyed by the Japanese government. Over the decades, some would try to atone for what they did, and some of their children would call for a more open discussion about what happened so that people could avoid committing similar crimes in the future.

The International Military Tribunal for the Far East: Determining Who Was Responsible

The US government appointed General Douglas MacArthur to head the occupation of Japan, which took place from 1945 to 1952. Among his responsibilities was to establish a war justice system to try the Japanese for their war crimes. In May 1946, the International Military Tribunal for the Far East was held in Tokyo. By this time, the Nuremberg trials had already established the procedures to be used, so MacArthur and other leaders used this as a template to indict twenty-eight Japanese, which included both members of the military and governmental figures. They were charged with crimes against peace (a charge that included their aggressive invasion of neighboring countries), crimes against humanity, and war crimes. However, there have been many who criticized the small number of Japanese people who ended up facing trial when there were so many more who should have been included. As John Dower would later describe the way people were chosen to be held accountable, the focus was on a few select people. The Japanese military police were not tried, the industrialists who encouraged and profited from the war were not tried, members of secret societies were not tried, and scientists who committed atrocities that rivaled what the Germans had done were not tried. Perhaps the most notable absence, though, was the Imperial family—not even Emperor Hirohito was tried for what his nation had done in his name. The rationale for this came from General MacArthur, who wanted to stabilize the nation as quickly as possible. The US felt the best way to do that was to leave the emperor as the head of the government. The people, particularly soldiers, had acted in his name, so it was hoped that his continued presence as their leader would help the Japanese to accept their defeat and the American occupation. The Far East Tribunal was also not focused solely on what happened in Nanjing, but it was one of the primary events that were scrutinized.

Unlike the Nuremberg trials, the Far East Tribunal was largely trying people for failing to act, known as crimes of omission. General Matsui Iwane and Hirota Koki (the foreign minister when the atrocities occurred) were perhaps the two people most targeted for crimes of omissions, as they had failed to control the soldiers. The prosecution gave evidence that both men knew what was happening in Nanjing but did not take actions to prevent the activities from occurring for far too long. Both men were convicted, with Hirota's judgment being particularly scathing:

> The tribunal is of the opinion that Hirota was derelict in his duty in not insisting before the Cabinet that immediate action be taken to put an end to the atrocities, failing any other action open to him to bring about the same result. He was content to rely on assurances which he knew were not being implemented while hundreds of murders, violations of women, and other atrocities were being committed daily. His inaction amounted to criminal negligence.
>
> -   International Military Tribunal for the Far East: Judgement of 4 November 1948

It was much easier to hold General Matsui accountable, as he was the commander of the efforts in Nanjing and had been present for the duration of the atrocities. General Matsui had certainly been the commander of the troops, but he had been too ill to lead them into the city. This does not absolve him of the atrocities, though, as he knew about what was happening and did not stop it. The attacks lasted six weeks, even as the foreigners in the Safety Zone repeatedly asked for intervention. Hirota had been responsible for the response, and he chose to do nothing for more than a month.

All twenty-eight people who were charged were convicted. Seven of them (including Matsui and Hirota) were convicted of the most serious crimes and were sentenced to hang. The other Japanese who were convicted were given jail sentences. Two of the twenty-eight men had died prior to the end of the tribunal, and one was found to be insane.

The seven men were executed on December 23rd, 1948.

There has been a lot of criticism for the trials, especially considering the atrocities that took place in Nanjing. It was felt by critics (especially the Chinese) that not enough people were held accountable, and the trials appeared to be more for show than a way of actually holding the Japanese accountable. The comparable trials against the Germans included 199 defendants and 161 convictions, with 37 criminals receiving a death sentence for their crimes. By comparison, the Japanese seemed to have largely gotten away with some of the worst war crimes in modern history.

This apparent bias was likely a result of the American leaders wanting to start implementing democracy in Japan with minimal resistance. With World War II over, they no longer viewed the Japanese as their enemies; the Chinese and Soviets were. This likely played a significant role in the lack of convictions. They didn't want to alienate the Japanese. Americans also played a large role in establishing education during their occupation, and the atrocities committed by the Japanese were largely omitted from the curriculum.

John Rabe

The role that John Rabe played during the preparation of the Imperial Army's arrival through the post-war events seems to be a contradiction to most people. He had only been in Nanjing to work as a teacher. He worked for the German company Siemens, and by 1931, he was helping to establish phone lines across the city. He and his family lived in a comfortable home that would eventually be located in the Safety Zone. In 1934, Rabe started a German school, which he held in his home. While acting as the chairman of the school board, he became a member of the Nazi Party (he had not lived in Germany since 1908). He would remain faithful to the party throughout the entire war, but it was very likely he had no idea what the party was doing in Europe since he had not been to Germany in decades. He flew the Nazi flag proudly over his home and school and also had a Nazi flag draped over his car. Rabe would have likely been a very easily identifiable figure in the city even before it became clear that a war was coming.

Rabe had chosen to stay in the city and had been instrumental in ensuring that the Safety Zone was established before the Imperial Army arrived. He had actively worked to protect soldiers who sought to hide from the Japanese, especially as it became clear that they would all be executed. Rabe's role in helping the people cannot be overstated, and he seemed to make it his mission to keep the people safe. The correspondence that he sent would be used to help convict Japanese military officials and leaders, even as the Nazi Party was being held accountable for their atrocities in Europe.

Once the Safety Zone was dissolved, the Siemens company told him to return home. They had heard about how he had led the people within the zone, and they may have wanted him to take a leadership role within the company. He did not receive such a role, but he did give lectures about what he had seen, including photographs and films that the Japanese had not managed to take from him. The German Gestapo stopped him when he returned to Berlin, and it was only because of the intervention of Siemens that he was able to keep his evidence.

When World War II ended, Rabe was denounced for his participation in the Nazi Party. The Soviet enforcement agency called the NKVD arrested him for this. They investigated him, but when that ended, they discharged him. Unfortunately, soon after, he was released, and the British Army arrested him. He went through the same process once again and was eventually discharged. About a year after the war in Europe ended, the Allies declared that he had been successfully "de-Nazified," but he was not given his full pension. The last few years of his life, Rabe was relatively poor, and it was only due to the parcels that the Chinese government sent him, along with some recompense, that he was able to keep going. He died in January of 1949 at the age of sixty-five. He was buried in Berlin, where Germans and Chinese still visit the grave to remember him. His headstone was later moved to the Nanjing Massacre Memorial.

Chapter 18 – The Memorial Hall of the Victims in Nanjing

While the events of that six-week period were well documented, they were largely ignored for decades. However, the Chinese survivors did not forget what had happened. The Nanjing Municipal Government built a memorial for the victims in 1985 in Jiangdongmen (one of the locations where mass executions were carried out and bodies were buried). It was called the Memorial Hall to the Victims in the Nanjing Massacre by Japanese Invaders.

The memorial was expanded in 1995, then again between 2005 and 2007, and today, it includes seventy-four thousand square meters. The outside portion of the memorial has exhibits that reflect the indignation and grief that the period caused, and it includes depictions of both life and death, with statues and carvings depicting the scenes of lost lives among the beautiful cypresses and pines. One of the monuments includes an engraving of the date the Japanese entered the city and the date when they left, at the end of January the following year. Another marble memorial includes some of the names of the victims, as well as the number 300,000, which is one of the most common estimates for the number of Chinese who were killed in Nanjing. Visitors can walk among the outdoor memorials to reflect on how so many people senselessly lost their lives to the invading Japanese army.

The exhibits were divided into three parts: an outdoor exhibit for reflection, the bones of some of the victims, and historical documents from the period.

The bones were excavated from the area when the memorial was made. This part of the exhibit includes coffins in which the bones rest. More than two hundred bones were found during an excavation in 1998. A second area is partially underground and displays roughly one thousand items that recall the tragedies that occurred during that brief period of time. Images taken during the events of that six-week period are displayed on the walls. There are also film documentaries that detailed what life was like for the Nanjing citizens who were trapped within the city.

For the 70th anniversary of the arrival of the Japanese in the city (December 13th, 2007), a new hall was open to the public. This part of the memorial was built to look like a ship's bow, as a way of representing "the Ship of Peace." When a person looks at the new addition in profile, it looks more like a broken saber. When looking directly down at the memorial, it appears to be a sword that transforms into a plowshare.

The purpose of the memorial is to remember those who died and to remind people of what can be done during war and how people who would be reluctant to even kill a snake in their garden back home can be worked into a frenzy. It attempts to educate people, not to sustain animosity toward the nation that perpetrated the crimes but to remind people that they cannot let it happen again. With some people trying to deny that any such event occurred or claiming that it wasn't as bad as the Chinese say, it is a way of showing that the facts were not inventions of anyone's imagination but real accounts of what happened.

Ultimately, the large memorial attempts to remind people that the world is not so far removed from some of the worst atrocities it has seen. It is more about prevention through education, as well as serving as a way of honoring and remembering those who lost their lives.

Chapter 19 – How the Atrocities Were Reported and Resulting Controversies

In the decades since 1938, the Rape of Nanjing has been revisited by survivors, perpetrators, and nations around the world.

How the US Reported the Rape of Nanjing

In the US, the horrors at Shanghai and Nanjing would be used to help stir up sentiment against the Japanese (this happened a few years before Pearl Harbor united the nation against the Axis Powers). Americans lived in Shanghai and Nanjing, and they were among the people who sent word back to their families, the Japanese Embassy, and other governmental figures in the hopes that something would be done to stop the tragedy from unfolding in Nanjing. The American diplomat in the city reported back to the US what he had heard from witnesses. However, it was the American journalists who chose to remain that reported back to news agencies in the US, detailing how the carnage began and was sustained for what felt like forever. The days bled into each other as Japanese soldiers killed indiscriminately, and the screams of women being abducted, raped, and murdered were a constant part of the city's noise.

There were reporters present from several prominent US and British news agencies, such as Archibald Trojan Steele (*Chicago Daily News*), Frank Tillman Durdin (*New York Times*), Arthur von Briesen Menken (Paramount Newsreel), Leslie C. Smith (Reuters), and Charles Yates McDaniel (Associated Press). These five reporters began to send back word of what they saw, though they were unable to send anything during the worst periods of the massacre. Their goal was to let the rest of the world know about the crimes the Japanese were perpetrating as the Second Sino-Japanese War began.

Steele had left Shanghai on the USS *Oahu* and returned to the ship after witnessing the atrocities of those early days. He was able to convince the radio operator on the gunboat to send a cable back to Chicago. On December 15th, 1937, the *Chicago Daily News* broke the story, writing, "Nanking's fall is a story of indescribable panic and confusion among the entrapped Chinese defenders, followed by a reign of terror by the conquering army that cost thousands of lives, many of them innocent ones." This was only two days after the Japanese entered the city, yet their behavior had already horrified those who witnessed it. Menken soon sent his own report to the *Seattle Daily Times* from the same vessel.

The other three journalists found other ways to cable back their own reports to their respective employers. From the very beginning of the atrocities, there were witnesses who reported back to the media, making it impossible for the Japanese to control the narrative around the rest of the world. Some of these reporters would continue to report what they had seen even after leaving Nanjing. Other Americans (not members of any news agency) continued to send reports from within the city as well. As they were unable to leave, they continued to record what they saw, eventually finding ways to get their information out to the world.

Many of the Westerners actually tried to get their reports out, but reports back to Europe were not quite as sensational, as the continent was already tense from Germany's actions during the late 1930s. Some of the stories from the US were reported in Europe. Not all of the reporters were American either, though their stories were printed on several continents.

How Japan Reported the Events of Nanjing

Due to their tight control over the way their soldiers' behavior was reported, the Japanese military and government ensured that none of the atrocities were reported. News of what was unfolding in Nanjing reached Japanese authorities quickly, as the Westerners who had remained sent messages to both the Japanese and their own nations in the hope that someone would end the atrocities.

The soldiers would be too ashamed to talk about what they had done even years after the events. When they did talk, they often seemed detached from the events, as if they knew how they would be judged for their actions.

While the Japanese citizens were aware of the events of the tribunal, the full extent of the war crimes and crimes against humanity were not detailed to them. This would have some serious repercussions later, as Japanese civilians would remain ignorant of the events. Due to this, some would be less willing to believe the recorded details. Similar to how Germans who had not seen the atrocities carried out by the Nazis would not believe reports, the Japanese could not see how their military would do anything so atrocious. The difference was the way that the two Axis Powers would eventually teach their younger generations about World War II. Today, German schools highlight how important it is to remember what they had done so they (or anyone else) would not do it again. By comparison, many Japanese citizens know about the tragedy that occurred in Nanjing, but they don't understand or believe the full scope of what took place. The US did not help, as it failed to take a similar approach as the

Germans when it came to teaching the Japanese, even though the US controlled nearly every aspect of Japanese life during the occupation. However, the German curriculum following the war had a lot of input from the nations that Germany had attacked, so it is understandable that they were more transparent and accurate in their portrayal of their role.

The Nazi Party had taken a very similar approach in masking its atrocities, but the two very different approaches to educating future generations would result in two very different perceptions of the war.

Japanese Recognition of Their Crimes

The Japanese government has not entirely faced their history head-on the way the Germans did (though it can be argued that the Germans had a lot more pressure to do so following World War II). Japan did not even publicly acknowledge what had happened until 1972. Prime Minister Tanaka Kakuei issued a statement to the People's Republic of China, saying, "[We are] keenly conscious of the responsibility for the serious damage that Japan caused in the past to the Chinese people through war, and deeply reproaches itself." It was short of an apology and failed to acknowledge any of the events for which Japan was said to reproach itself.

During the 1980s, Emperor Hirohito spoke to South Korean President Chun Doo Hwan, expressing his own personal regret. "It is indeed regrettable that there was an unfortunate past between us for a period in this century and I believe that it should not be repeated again." Later in the year, Japanese Prime Minister Nakasone Yasuhiro would express similar regret for what had happened by "unleashing of rampant ultra-nationalism and militarism and the war that brought great devastation of the people of many countries around the world and to our country as well."

For the 50th anniversary of the start of the war (August 1995), the Japanese prime minister issued Japan's first official statement of regret, saying that the Japanese needed to atone for what it had done in the past. Several more apologies have been issued in the years since, with the most recent being made by Prime Minister Abe Shinzo. With his last apology, Abe expressed a desire to stop apologizing, saying, "We must not let our children, grandchildren, and even further generations to come, who have nothing to do with that war, be predestined to apologize." Following this, he did say that Japanese citizens needed to be aware of their past, even if they shouldn't keep apologizing for it.

Controversies

Just as there are Holocaust deniers today, there are people who deny that the events in Nanjing occurred or that they were not nearly as horrific as some people claim. In addition to some claiming that the images were doctored to make the Japanese look worse, there are claims that the reports about Nanjing were specifically biased against the Japanese. Over the last few decades, deniers have called books and other media that discuss the atrocities as propaganda that are meant to turn people against the Japanese.

While a lot of the film footage and images were authentic, there were some that were doctored or entirely faked by the Chinese and Americans. With there being a reported 200,000 living in Nanjing before the war, the reports of more than 300,000 people being killed are questionable. There were soldiers and other people who sought refuge in the city, but the entire Chinese population in the city was not killed (though a significant portion of the population was killed, as the immediate investigation showed). It is possible that some events of the Nanjing Massacre were exaggerated, but that is the problem. The numbers and a few events may have been exaggerated, but even the Japanese soldiers themselves and their own photographs prove that the atrocities were very real. Too many reports from the neutral

Westerners in the city, particularly the pleas from John Rabe himself, showed that it was a nightmarish chapter in the city's history.

The events of Nanjing definitely did happen, but it is also easy to understand the concern that people might be trying to create a wave of anti-Japanese sentiment. During World War II, the US established their own concentration camps for Japanese-Americans; there were no such camps for the Germans. In Europe, the reports from Nanjing made many Europeans very anti-Japanese. This is more a symptom of another problem. Even though the Germans have taught their citizens about the horrors the Nazis committed, the Germans were vilified for decades after World War II. Anything associated with Germans was treated as dangerous. For example, German Shepherds, Doberman Pinschers, and Rottweilers had long been desirable breeds, but this changed after World War II. While they are great guard dogs, their German roots vilified the breeds. They were depicted as dangerous dogs who were more likely to kill people. Because of this, they were (and still are) on banned dog breed lists in different communities around the world. This kind of demonization of a people is not abnormal, as it has happened time and time again in history. Thus, it is easy to understand the concern that detailing atrocities could turn people against an entire nation. There remains a fairly anti-Japanese sentiment in many other Asian nations even today.

However, it is important to take an approach that is similar to the memorial in Nanjing. History should be taught in a way that is both accurate and instructional. It shouldn't be used to justify future atrocities or biases. Denying that something happened is just as harmful as using history to vilify an entire people.

All nations are guilty of atrocities against other groups of people, even today. Accountability and accuracy are important for proper education to prevent similar massacres in the future.

Conclusion

During the Second Sino-Japanese War, Japan attempted to expand its empire across the Asian continent. Like their German allies, the Japanese were experiencing a particularly violent form of nationalism, with many believing that they were superior to all other Asian nations and the Japanese military being particularly insistent that no other nation could defeat them. A lot of this could be attributed to how successful they had been when fighting against China and Russia, and this likely helped them to start viewing people of other nations as being lesser.

Their dehumanization would result in one of the worst atrocities of the war when the Japanese decided to invade Nanjing. As they made their way across the mainland, the Japanese military did not differentiate between the people in the Chinese military and the Chinese citizens. At the time, China's capital was Nanjing, making it an obvious target for a Japanese attack. The Chinese government began an evacuation, getting many of their most important figures out of the city before the Japanese reached it, but many citizens could not escape.

When the Japanese arrived in Nanjing in December 1937, they immediately began a massacre that was unbelievable. The barbarism enacted against the Chinese indicated that the Japanese didn't even see the citizens as people. Lining people up and slaughtering them in a grotesque competition, raping citizens before killing them, looting the homes of the people they killed, and destroying over a third of the city's buildings were some of the most heinous acts of the Japanese military, but there were many other atrocities that they enacted upon the civilians. They branched out to destroy surrounding towns, ensuring that no one would stand against them when they established the city as the capital for their puppet government.

When World War II finally ended, the men who ordered the attacks were tried and convicted of war crimes, but this did not make up for the actions they had done. One of the reasons that the Nanjing Massacre Memorial was created was to remember the lives that were senselessly lost over that six-week period. The atrocities at Nanjing were just as horrific as the tragedies of the Holocaust, but until more recently, it has not been as widely discussed. It is important to remember these kinds of atrocities to help ensure people are aware and so similar atrocities aren't committed in the future.

Here's another book by Captivating History that you might like

Free Bonus from Captivating History (Available for a Limited time)

Hi History Lovers!

Now you have a chance to join our exclusive history list so you can get your first history ebook for free as well as discounts and a potential to get more history books for free! Simply visit the link below to join.

Captivatinghistory.com/ebook

Also, make sure to follow us on Facebook, Twitter and Youtube by searching for Captivating History.

Bibliography

10 Facts about the Second Sino-Japanese War, Sophie Gee, HistoryHit, October 23, 2020, www.historyhit.com/

A Question of Morality: John Rabe, Facing History and Ourselves, April 11, 2021, www.facinghistory.org/

An Epidemic in Lu Chow Fu – A Glimpse of Mission Work in 1900's China, China Change, February 20, 2012, chinachange.org/2012/02/20/

Brief History of Nanjing, XU Chengyan, ISLS Organizing Committee, March 5, 2017, www.nfls.com.cn/isls/

Bushido: The Ancient Code of the Samurai Warrior, Edward Drea, Greg Bradsher Robert Hanyok, James Lide, Michael Petersen, Daqing Yang, March 22, 2021, Nazi War Crimes and Japanese Imperial Government Records Interagency Working Group, Washington DC, www.archives.gov/

Did It Really Help to Be a Japanese Colony? East Asian Economic Performance in Historical Perspective, Anne Booth, May 2, 2007, The Asia-Pacific Journal, apjjf.org/-Anne-Booth/2418/article.html

First Sino-Japanese War, Editors of Encyclopedia Britannica, Encyclopedia Britannica, March 1,

2021, https://www.britannica.com/event/First-Sino-Japanese-War-1894-1895

How Japan Tried to Save Thousands of Jews from the Holocaust, Kevin McGeary, March 28, 2019, Los Angeles Review of Books China Channel, chinachannel.org/

Iris Chang, *The Rape of Nanking: The Forgotten Holocaust,* December 1991, Basic Books

Japan, China, the United States and the Road to Pearl Harbor, 1937-41, Office of the Historian, Foreign Service Institute, United States Department of State, March 1, 2021, https://history.state.gov/milestones/1937-1945/pearl-harbor

Japanese Crimes in Nanjing, 1937-38: A Reappraisal, Jean-Louis Margolin, OpenEdition Journals. Accessed January 2, 2021, journals.openedition.org/

Japanese Imperialism and the Road to War, Facing History and Ourselves, March 1, 2021, https://www.facinghistory.org/resource-library/teaching-nanjing-atrocities/japanese-imperialism-and-road-war

Nanjing Massacre: Chinese History, The Editors of Encyclopedia Britannica, Britannica, March 2, 2021, www.britannica.com/event/Nanjing-Massacre

Researching Japanese War Crimes, Edward Drea, Greg Bradsher Robert Hanyok, James Lide, Michael Petersen, Daqing Yang, March 22, 2021, Nazi War Crimes and Japanese Imperial Government Records Interagency Working Group, Washington DC, www.archives.gov/

Second Sino-Japanese War, Editors of Encyclopedia Britannica, Encyclopedia Britannica, March 1, 2021, https://www.britannica.com/event/Second-Sino-Japanese-War

Seeds of Unrest: The Taiping Movement, Facing History and Ourselves, March 2, 2021, www.facinghistory.org/nanjing-atrocities/

Shanghai 1937: This Is China's Forgotten Stalingrad, Michael Peck, May 30, 2016, The National Interest, nationalinterest.org/

Sino-Japanese Relations: Issues for U.S. Policy, Emma Chanlett-Avery, Kerry Dumbaugh, William H.
Cooper, Congressional Research Service, December 19, 2008, https://fas.org/sgp/crs/row/R40093.pdf

The Marco Polo Bridge Incident, Kallie Szczepanski, November 17, 2019, Thought Co., www.thoughtco.com/

The Nanjing Massacre: A Japanese Journalist Confronts Japan's National Shame, Honda Katsuichi, 1999, M.E. Sharpe, Taylor & Francis

The Nanking Massacre, 1937, Kallie Szczepanski, Thought Co, March 6, 2017, www.thoughtco.com/

The Rape of Nanking or Nanjing Massacre (1937), Historical Work Material, March 3, 2021, www.pacificwar.org.au/

The Story of the Royal Ulster Rifleman and the Battle of Shanghai, History, March 20, 2021, Sky History, www.history.co.uk/

War Zone – City of Terror: The Japanese Takeover of Shanghai, Military History Matters, February 8, 2013, Currently Publishing, www.military-history.org/

What Motivated Japanese Aggression in World War II?, Kallie Szczepanski, July 27, 2019, Thought Co,www.thoughtco.com/

Who Were the Comfort Women? The Establishment of Comfort Stations, Digital Museum, March 22, 2021, Asian Women's Fund, www.awf.or.jp/e1/facts-01.html

Why Japanese Forces Showed "No Mercy" during the Fall of Shanghai, Warfare History Network, May 10, 2020, The National Interest, nationalinterest.org/

The Nanjing Atrocities Reported in the U.S. Newspapers, 1937-38, Suping Lu, April 12, 2021, Readex, www.readex.com/

International Military Tribunal for the Far East: Judgement of 4 November 1948, John Pritchard, Sonia M. Zaide, Vol. 22, April 12, 2021, crimeofaggression.info/documents/6/1948_Tokyo_Judgment.pdf

Memorial Hall to the Victims in the Nanjing Massacre, Travel China Guide, April 8, 2021, www.travelchinaguide.com/

First Battle of Shanghai; 28 Jan 1932 – 8 Mar 1932, C. Pen Chen, March 20, 2021, World War II, ww2db.com/

Second Battle of Shanghai; 13 Aug 1937 – 9 Nov 1937, C. Pen Chen, March 20, 2021, World War II, ww2db.com/

The Shanghai Incident, 1932, PE Matt, February 7, 2015, Pacific Eagles WWII Pacific War Combat, pacificeagles.net/

Samurai and Bushido, History.com Editors, August 21, 2018, History, www.history.com/

Nanking Massacre, History.com Editors, June 7, 2019, History.com, www.history.com/

Japanese War Crimes Trial Begins, History, July 28, 2019, A&E Television Networks, www.history.com/

The First Sino-Japanese War, Kallie Szczepanski, October 17, 2019, Thought Co, www.thoughtco.com/

A Brief History of Manchuria, Kallie Szczepanski, January 5, 2020, Thought Co., www.thoughtco.com/

Credibility and End of the League, The National Archives, March 19, 2021, www.nationalarchives.gov.uk/

Japan-China Friendship Office, Rawfish-Maguro, MIT, March 1, 2021, http://www.mit.edu/course/17/17.s21/maguro.old/friends_home.html

Nanjing History, Travel China Guide, March 1, 2021, www.travelchinaguide.com/

Sino-Japanese War: WW2, Sky History, AE Networks, March 3, 2021, www.history.co.uk/

The Second Sino-Japanese War, Alpha History, March 3, 2021, alphahistory.com/

BRIA 18 3b The "Rape of Nanking," Constitutional Rights Foundation, April 11, 2021, Civics Renewal Network, www.crf-usa.org/bill-of-rights-in-action/

Japanese Invade Manchuria, History Central, March 19, 2021, www.historycentral.com/

Battle of Shanghai, Yuen, Tony, Iris, March 20, 2021, Nanking Massacre: The Untold Story, depts.washington.edu/

The Road to Nanking, Walter Zapotoczny Jr., March 21, 2021, Warfare History Network, warfarehistorynetwork.com/

Wang Ching-wei, Your Dictionary, April 2021, https://biography.yourdictionary.com/

Geneva Conventions: 1864-1977, Malcom Shaw, April 11, 2021, Britannica, www.britannica.com/

Nanking Massacre, Wikipedia, April 11, 2021, www2.gvsu.edu/